The
ABC
of
STAGE
TECHNOLOGY

Francis Reid

D0543063

A & C Black · London
Heinemann · New Hampshire

First published 1995
A & C Black (Publishers) Limited
35 Bedford Row, London WC1R 4JH

ISBN 0–7136–4055–3

© 1995 Francis Reid

Published simultaneously in the USA by Heinemann
A division of Reed Elsevier, Inc.
361 Hanover Street
Portsmouth, NH 03801–3912
Offices and Agents throughout the world

Distributed in Canada by Reed Books Canada,
75 Clegg Road, Markham, Ontario L6G 1A1

ISBN 0–435–08684–7

CIP catalogue records for this book are available from the British
Library and the Library of Congress.

Typeset in 10 on 11 Gill by Florencetype Ltd, Stoodleigh, Devon
Printed in Great Britain by Biddles Ltd, Guildford, Surrey

Prologue

I hope that this glossary will help those who wish to develop their understanding of theatre technology or to improve their communication with the specialists who practice its mysteries.

Theatrespeak is becoming increasingly uniform in all English language countries, but an attempt has been made to incorporate significant national differences where these still exist. When alternatives are only a matter of spelling, the English of England has been adopted – *theatres* and *colours* rather than *theaters* and *colors*. To avoid the text being peppered with 'qv', cross references have been restricted to occasions when the connection with another entry is not particularly obvious. Readers uncertain about the meaning of any technical term used in the text should seek an explanation under the individual alphabetical entry for that term.

All entries represent my own understanding of what the words mean and reflect my own use of them. Although working backstage for over forty years and trying to teach the subject for nearly as long, I have never undertaken any formal theatre studies. Consequently, it is quite probable that my personal vocabulary has acquired not just minor inaccuracies but major misconceptions. Furthermore, since theatre is a people industry, it is inevitable that some of the text may be coloured by personal experiences and opinions. In the interest of my own education and in anticipation of a second edition, I invite corrections for existing entries and suggestions for additional ones.

For illustrations I am particularly indebted to ASG, Denis Diderot, Drottningholm Court Theatre, Hall Harkness Ltd, Albert A Hopkins, Jean-Pierre Moynet, Clive Odam, Arthur Pougin, Robin Rae, RHWL Architects, Roscolab Ltd, Royal Opera House, Clarkson Stanfield, Strand Lighting Archive, William Lewis Telbin, Theatre Museum, James Thomas Engineering Ltd, Triple E Engineering Ltd and the many technicians who have allowed their work to be invaded by my camera.

Abseiling This technique, developed by mountaineers for lowering themselves down steep vertical surfaces using a rope attached above and secured around the body, has been adapted by theatre technicians for difficult rigging situations.

Mountaineering techniques in use for rigging.

The technique is of particular value in non-orthodox situations where the absence of a fly tower requires temporary facilities to be built upwards with trussing from stage floor level. Abseiling requires suitable harnesses and special training in the use of the equipment and its safety procedures.

ABTT (Assocation of British Theatre Technicians) A society of all those who support the actor. Through meetings, publications and specialist committees, the ABTT provides architects, designers and technicians with a forum for exchanging information and opinion. The ABTT is the British arm of OISTAT. See also USITT.

Acrylics Acrylic plastics, clear or coloured, transparent or translucent, are relatively easily worked with standard tools used at slow speeds. The material is available in most three-dimensional formats but the most common stage use is in sheet form for transparent windows and translucent floors.

Act as known Contractual term for a variety (vaudeville) act who will insert their own material (script, music, action, props, etc.) into the production for an agreed length, timed in minutes.

Act drop (Act curtain) A curtain, other than the main house curtain, used to signify beginnings and ends of acts. Formerly there was often a special curtain which was part of the theatre's equipment, but now it is usually specially designed for the production.

Acting area The area, within the stage setting, where the actors perform.

Acts (1) Divisions of a play, in today's practice normally those commencing or ending with an interval in the performance. (2) Self-contained performances by variety (vaudeville) actors. See also FRONTCLOTH and OLIO.

Air castors Small skirted pads which, on filling with compressed air, enable scenery to be moved easily by floating it on the hovercraft principle. When the compressed air is removed the weight of the scenery ensures that it sits very firmly on the stage floor. Also used to move sections of auditorium around in multiform theatres. For successful operation, floor surfaces must be very smooth and even.

Alive Sometimes just LIVE. Any prop or piece of scenery still to be used or re-used during the remainder of the current performance.

Amphitheatre Strictly speaking, as derived from the Roman *anfiteatro*, a large auditorium for spectacular productions, usually in the open air, with an oval performing area surrounded by tiered audience seating. Sometimes used loosely, but wrongly, for Greek and Roman theatres with 180° seating.

The original ASPHALEIA STAGE.

Anilyne dyes Transparent dyes used for painting cloths and gauzes. Since they stain the material rather than adhere to its surface, they do not enhance the texture in the way that paint pigments do. Consequently, the surface tends to be rather flat and difficult to light. Moreover, the depth of dye penetration makes alterations virtually impossible.

Anticipate Giving a cue momentarily early so that the effect of the cue coincides with a precise moment of stage action, words or music. The anticipation may be as short as an actor's intake of breath or a musician's upbeat.

Appearance money Additional payments made to technical crew who are required to move scenery or props in view of the audience.

Apron (1) Area of stage projecting towards or into the auditorium. In proscenium theatres, the part of the stage (also known as the FORESTAGE) in front of the main house curtain. (2) Black border hung from the fly gallery to complete the wing masking.

Arbor Counterweight cradle. (US)

Arena A large performance space within a large capacity auditorium where the seating almost or totally surrounds the acting area.

Asbestos Prior to realisation of its toxic dangers, asbestos was used to increase fire resistance of safety curtains which were consequently often referred to colloquially as 'the asbestos', especially in the US.

ASM Assistant stage manager.

Asphaleian system A type of stage construction pioneered by the Asphaleian Company's 1884 installation in the Budapest Opera House. Using steel to reduce fire risk, the stage floor was divided into a series of platforms which could be raised, lowered or tilted by hydraulic pistons. See page 3.

Backcloth (Backdrop) A full width, full height, painted cloth at the back of the stage, completing the depth of the scene.

Backflap A hinge capable of being turned back on itself. Used for joining scenic flats together, either permanently so that the painted faces close together like the pages of a book or, with a removable pin (see PIN HINGE), so that they may be moved and stored independently.

Backing (1) Scenery behind an opening such as a door, window, fireplace, etc. (2) The money invested in a commercial production.

Back of house A fairly new term, probably coined by architects, for all those non-public areas not covered by the long established term FRONT OF HOUSE. Those who work back of house still seem to favour the traditional, but perhaps looser, BACKSTAGE.

Back painting Dense opaque neutral paint applied to the back of painted scenic canvas to prevent light bleeding through from behind.

Backstage All the non-audience areas beyond the proscenium.

Back wall The structural wall at the rear of the stage area. Often painted black to assist masking and to minimise light reflections. If this wall is a plain surface free from pipes, radiators, etc., it is sometimes plastered and painted white (preferably with the palest of light blue tints added) for use as a sky.

Bar Fixed or flown, steel or alloy, tubing from which scenery or lighting may be suspended. (**Pipe** in US)

Bare stage A stage completely free from any scenery.

Barre Horizontal support rail used by dancers when practising. Ballet companies visiting theatres without suitable rehearsal rooms set up temporary barres on the stage for daily class which then has to be slotted into the technical operations schedule.

Barrel The word *bar* is a contraction of the gas barrel which was originally used as pipe for suspension.

Barrel clamp A clamp used to fix scenery or lights to a bar. (**Pipe clamp** in US)

Barrel slings Short lengths of chain with a snap hook at one end, used for hanging battened cloths from the bars of a flying system.

Bastard prompt A theatre where the stage manager's desk for cueing and prompting is situated OP (opposite prompt side, i.e. stage right facing the audience) rather than PS (prompt side, i.e. stage left facing the audience). The reason is usually architectural due to an irregularly shaped stage or to convenience of dressing room access. Most new or refurbished theatres now have a mobile stage manager's desk with power and communication multicore cables which allow it to be plugged either side.

Batten (1) Lengths of timber at the tops and bottoms of cloths. (2) Timber used for joining flats together (BATTENING OUT) for flying as a french flat.

Batten clamp A metal clamp for attaching the timber battens of flown scenery to fly bars (pipes). Some types of clamp allow a cloth to be shortened by rolling on the batten before clamping.

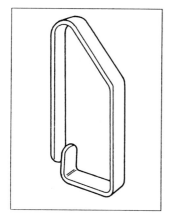

BATTEN CLAMP (left) used (right) to hang a cloth which has been shortened by rolling.

Battening out Joining flats together in preparation for flying by screwing timber battens across them.

Bauprobe A full scale mock-up of a proposed scene design on the stage. This 'build rehearsal' enables experiments to be made with minor variations in dimensions in an endeavour to use existing elevators, stock rostra, treads, etc. It also allows the director and choreographer to confirm the suitability of the form and size of the acting area.

Bays Acting areas as wide as the stage and as deep as the distance between adjacent wings and borders. Bays are numbered from downstage to upstage.

Beat A measure of the shortest variation in time by which a stage manager advances or delays the calling of a cue. It may be as long as the beat in a bar of music or as short as an almost imperceptible intake of breath.

Beginners The call for actors involved at the start of the first scene to come to the stage. Usually called by the stage manager five minutes before the anticipated time of 'curtain up' on the performance.

Belaying pin One of the many terms carried over from sailing ship rigging to theatre rigging. A vertical pin of wood or metal, slotted into the horizontal fly rail, to which rope lines are tied (belayed). See also PIN RAIL and CLEAT.

Billy block A pulley, attached by a short length of rope, used for such minor temporary suspension as storing a prop by flying it out of the way in the wings. May also be used to divert the pull of a working line.

Black box Simple experimental performance space, painted black throughout for neutrality, where the relationship between acting and audience zones can be arranged in a wide range of alternative configurations.

Blacks Black masking in the form of leg and border curtains. These were traditionally made from velour gathered to provide fullness, but are now more commonly straight and utilise matt fabrics such as serge.

Black tat Small pieces of black fabric used to cover the back of joins in scenery where light might otherwise leak through. Usually fixed by stapling.

Bleed Lighting a scene behind a gauze to make the scene gradually visible through the gauze.

Block One or more sheaves (grooved pulley wheels) mounted in a wooden or metal framework.

Block and tackle An arrangement of pulleys and ropes designed to gain mechanical advantage by making the travel of the pulling line longer than the travel of the load.

Blues Tinted working lights in the wings, arranged to cast minimum spill on the acting area so that they may remain alive during performances.

Boards An older term for the stage, as in 'treading the boards'.

Boat truck See TRUCK.

Bobbinet A type of hexagonal open weave gauze lightweight cotton fabric. (US)

Bobbins Carriers on a tab track to which curtains are attached for horizontal movement. See also LEADING BOBBIN.

Bolton twill Cotton material with a diagonal texture used for black neutral masking.

Book (1) The words of a musical, particularly the story line rather than the lyrics of the songs. (2) The prompt copy is often referred to as 'the book'. (3) To fold a pair of hinged scenery book flats. (4) To contract an act or production for a date. (5) To buy a ticket for a given performance.

Book ceiling A horizontal ceiling built in two hinged sections so that it may be folded for raising into the flys.

Book flat A pair of scenic flats hinged together. When angled, the mutual support increases their stability, while folding paint to paint allows storage in a pack with reduced risk of damage to the decorative surfaces. Sometimes called Twofold.

Book wing Book flats at the side of the stage with one flat set on-and-off (i.e. parallel to the front of the stage), the other angled downstage to complete the masking.

Boom Vertical pipe, usually for mounting spotlights. The bottom is screwed to the stage and the top secured by a spot line.

Borders Strips of material, which may be neutral or carry a design, hung horizontally above the stage to form a limit to the scene and to mask the technical regions above the performance area. See also CUT BORDER and FRAMED BORDER.

Bosun's chair Wooden seat flown by a rope to enable a technician to carry out rigging and maintenance at inaccessible positions high above the stage.

Bottle screw See TURNBUCKLE.

Bounce Dropping the house curtain and immediately flying it out again without pause, while the actors are taking curtain calls (bows).

Bounce cloth (Bouncer) A plain white cloth hung upstage of a translucent (fabric or plastic) backcloth, particularly a skycloth, and used to light it from behind by reflection. A spare cloth, reverse hung so that the unpainted canvas back faces downstage, is often used.

Box office card A poster 15in × 10in, printed on card. The unprinted reverse of out-of-date box office cards was for many years the traditional surface for writing backstage plots.

Box set Naturalistic setting of a complete room built from flats with only the side nearest the audience (the 'fourth wall') missing. Often includes a ceiling.

Bows Acknowledging applause at the end of a performance. (US) See also CURTAIN CALL.

Brace See STAGE BRACE and FRENCH BRACE.

Brace cleat (Eye) Metal eye on a flat into which a stage brace may be hooked. Simple screw eyes are also used.

Brace jack US for FRENCH BRACE.

Brace weight Weight for securing the foot of a brace.

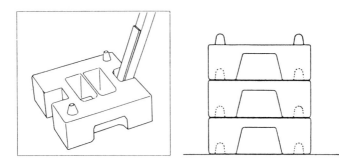

The weights used for holding BRACES firmly on the floor are cast in a format designed for ease in handling and stacking.

Brail To pull suspended scenery upstage or downstage from its natural free-hanging position by means of short rope lines attached to the ends of the fly bar.

Breakaway A prop specially designed and constructed to be broken during the action. Strictly speaking should be capable of being put together again for re-use at the next performance, but the term is also used for some plastic or sugar-glass breakables, such as bottles, which are not re-usable.

Breast To pull suspended scenery upstage or downstage from its natural free-hanging position by means of a rope line passed between fly floors and crossing the fly bar's suspension lines.

Bridges (1) Access catwalks passing across the stage or incorporated within the auditorium ceiling – often to facilitate spotlight focusing. (2) Elevators which can raise or sink sections of a stage floor.

An opera house false proscenium formed by a mobile lighting BRIDGE and tower structure, to provide an opening of adjustable height and width.

Bridle Ropes, wires or chains attached to two points on a flown piece in order to spread the load carried by a flying line.

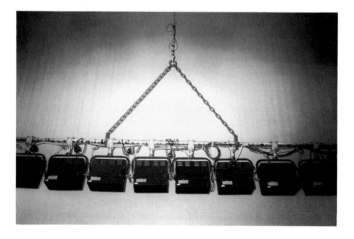

Spreading the load with a BRIDLE.

Bring it in Instruction to the fly crew to lower in a piece of scenery.

Bristle trap A small square trap, similar in function to a STAR TRAP. The hole in the stage surface is filled with bristles projecting inwards from the edges of the hole. The actor is propelled through the flexible bristles, thus appearing to emerge from a floor which immediately closes.

Build Constructing a scene from its constituent parts.

Built Scenery which is three-dimensional structures rather than two-dimensional paintings.

Bump in/out Australasian term for getting scenery in and out of a theatre. See GET-IN, GET-OUT, LOAD IN/OUT.

Bus and truck A tour specially designed for short stops, often of only one, two or three nights. (US)

Call (1) Notification of a working session (e.g. rehearsal call, band call, etc.). (2) Request for actors to come to the stage as their entrances are imminent (formerly given by a callboy, now by dressing room loudspeakers). (3) Acknowledgement of applause (e.g. curtain call).

Call board Backstage notice board where work schedules and notifications of rehearsal and performance calls are posted.

Cans Headsets with a single earpiece and integral boom microphone, used for communication.

CANS.

Canvas The heavy cotton fabric traditionally used for painted scenery, whether as hanging cloths and borders or covering the timber frames of flats. Most flats are now covered in 4mm or 6mm ply, although canvas or other textiles may be glued to this plywood backing to provide a texture for painting.

Capstan winch A winch with a vertical rotating drum and a series of horizontal bars. Rotated by several walking crew, a single winch could power the simultaneous substitution of all the wings in the chariots of eighteenth- and early nineteenth-century theatres.

The understage CAPSTAN WINCH at Drottningholm enables all seven pairs of wings to be replaced simultaneously.

Carpenter Apart from the obvious label for someone who constructs in wood, carpenter is used to describe experts in all aspects of scenery handling. See also MECHANIST.

Carpenter's scene Old name for a downstage scene, preferably noisy, played while a big complex scene was being set behind the frontcloth.

Carpet cut A narrow hinged trap along the full width of the front of the stage floor, used to clamp the front edge of a stagecloth (floorcloth) which is then stretched and tacked to the floor at the sides and rear. The trap is also useful for running cables from one side of the stage to the other. Often omitted from new stages.

Carpet hoist A method of transferring the counter-weighting load to an adjacent cradle when the load becomes out of balance because, for example, scenery has to be removed from the bar or the drift wires have to be slackened so that flown scenery may be set at an angle. See also OVERHAUL.

Castors (Casters) Small wheels on the bottom of scenery to assist movement. These may be fixed (i.e. straight), swivel or locking swivel, according to the control required. Castors are also available with a lifting mechanism which allows the scenery (usually a truck) to sit firmly on the floor until jacked up for movement on the wheels.

Casuals Part-time temporary staff.

Catwalk A narrow suspended walkway to provide access, particularly one spanning the stage from one fly floor to that on the other side.

Ceiling In some box sets the pursuit of realism is taken to the extent of providing a canvas ceiling over the major part of the set. Such a ceiling usually covers the upstage area, but leaves sufficient downstage space clear for the lighting. The ceiling is constructed of framed canvas and is flown on at least two sets of lines. If required to be set and struck in scene changes, the ceiling may be flown vertically on one set of lines, while the other set is attached as pick-up lines when horizontal hanging is required. See BOOK CEILING and ROLL CEILING.

Ceiling flipper A vertical piece attached to the downstage edge of a horizontal ceiling. When painted and preferably moulded, its design adds to the illusion of a ceiling. This illusion can be diminished by the alternative of a neutral masking border.

Ceiling plate A fitting with a ring for attaching a flying line to a ceiling.

Cellar The area under a trapped stage from which scenery and actors may appear and into which they may be lowered.

Centre The centre line (between the 'short' and the 'long') of a set of hemp flying lines.

Centre line An imaginary line from the front to the back of the stage through the exact centre of the proscenium opening.

Chain bag (Bucket) Canvas bag hung under a chain hoist to collect chain as it passes through the hoist mechanism.

Chain hoist Lifting device, manual or motor driven, using chain as its load bearing suspension line.

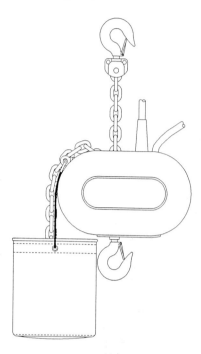

CHAIN HOIST with bucket. (Thomas CM Lodestar)

Chain pocket A continuous pocket sewn along the bottom of a soft fabric curtain or gauze to allow weighting so that it hangs smoothly without creases. Traditional chain is used for curtains which draw to the side but has been superseded by lengths of electrical conduit screwed together for flown pieces.

Chains (1) Short lengths of chain used to suspend battened cloths and borders from the bars of a counterweight flying system. (**Trim chains** in US) (2) Slender chain is sometimes used to weight the bottom of gauzes although lengths of screwed electric conduit tube are usually preferred to keep the gauze stretched.

Chalk line see SNAP LINE.

Chariots The understage wheeled carriages which supported and moved the wing flats in the slots of the stages of eighteenth- and early nineteenth-century theatres.

Check plot A plot which lists the position of each prop

or item of scenery at a given point during a performance. See also RUNNING PLOTS.

Cherry picker An access tower on a narrow wheeled base.

Choreographer Originally a person who creates dances but now widened to include anyone directing movement or responsible for the staging of musical numbers or sequences.

Clattercrash A device for making an extended crashing

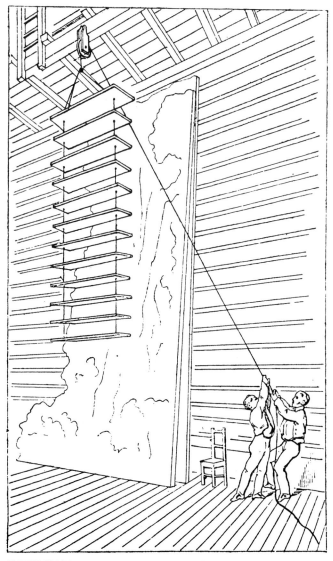

CLATTERCRASH.

sound. Although largely superseded by sound effects which have been electronically generated and/or recorded, still occasionally used for storms in conjunction with thunder sheets and drums.

Clear (1) Remove all props, etc. from the stage. (2) Instruction for everyone except the actors involved in the next scene to leave the stage because that scene is about to be revealed.

Clearing stick A long lightweight wooden pole used for separating high items of scenery which are interfering with each other – e.g. a border which has become trapped between flats.

Cleat Shaped piece of timber or metal for tying-off rope line – usually in the fly gallery or on the backs of scenic flats.

Cleat line A rope line, fixed to one scenic flat and passed over the cleat on another, allowing them to be quickly and firmly, but temporarily, joined together. Also known as LASH LINE and THROW LINE.

Clew Metal ring or triangle used to join several suspension ropes or wires to a single pulling line.

Four suspension lines joined by a swivelling CLEW to a single pulling line.

Cloth A large area of scenic canvas hanging vertically. (**Drop** in US) The top and sides are normally masked. A cloth may have wooden battens at top and bottom or cloth ties at the top and a sewn pocket for weighting (usually by conduit) at the bottom. A BACKCLOTH completes the rear of a scene. A FRONTCLOTH hangs well downstage, usually to hide a scene change taking place behind. See also CUT CLOTH.

Cloth rack Long shelving at the back of the stage, in a scene dock or under the stage (accessed by a cloth trap), for storage of scenic cloths rolled on their timber battens.

Cloth trap A long trap, the width of the stage, for lowering rolled cloths to storage racks under the stage. In large opera houses this trap may be a long narrow elevator.

Clove hitch The standard knot for fixing rope to a flying bar (pipe). Often completed with two half hitches. (*See illustration on page 51*.)

Come down (1) To move downstage, i.e. towards the audience. (2) Time of final curtain as in 'What time does the performance come down?'.

Commonsense A key skill required by anyone seeking a career in stage technology.

Conduit Lengths of narrow bore metal conduit tubing, as supplied for the protection of electrical wiring in permanent installations, used to weight the bottoms of cloths and gauzes. The threaded ends of the individual lengths are screwed together as they are slipped into the pocket sewn along the bottom.

Feeding screwed lengths of CONDUIT into the pocket at the bottom of a cloth.

Contour curtain A curtain with several vertical hoisting lines which allow sections to be raised differentially to produce swagging in alternative scalloped patterns.

Contra An account for materials supplied and services incurred by a theatre on behalf of a producing management. Normally settled by deduction from the producing manager's share of the box office receipts.

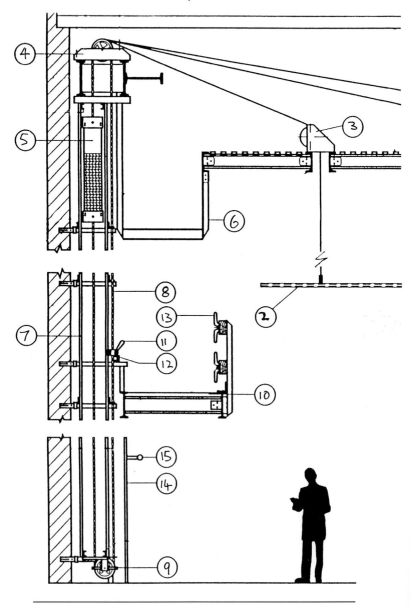

Corner block Triangular piece of plywood used to reinforce timber joints on flats.

Corner plate L-shaped metal plate used to reinforce timber joints on flats.

Corner traps Downstage traps, one towards each side of the stage, just wide enough for a single actor to appear or exit.

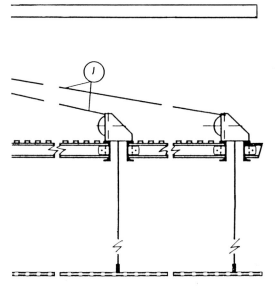

Basic structure of a single purchase COUNTERWEIGHT flying system. Lines (1) from the fly bar (2) pass over grid blocks (3) and head block (4) to the cradle (5) to which counterweights are added from the loading gallery (6). This counterweight cradle runs up and down the stage wall in guides (7) operated by a hauling line (8) passing around the bottom pulley (9). The hauling lines are operated by the fly crew on the fly floor (10) where there is a rope lock (11) for each line on the rail (12). There are also cleats (13) for tying off additional manually hauled hemp lines. At stage level there is a protective grill (14) and a rail (15) for packing flats against.

Corsican trap So called because it was first used in *The Corsican Brothers*. Also known as the Ghost Glide. A trap with a platform which moves across the stage as it rises, so that actors seem to glide across the stage as they appear through it.

Counterweights Iron weights which are placed in the cradles of a flying system to counterbalance the weight of flown scenery.

Cour Stage left (actor facing the audience) in the French theatre, derived from a tradition whereby the court was always to the left and the garden to the right. Hence stage right is JARDIN.

Cradle The frame for holding the weights in a counter-weight flying system. (**Arbor** in US)

Crew The technicians responsible for all the stage operations. Sometimes stage crew, fly crew, LX crew, etc.

Crossover (1) A passage immediately behind the back wall of the stage to allow rapid movement of actors and crew from one side of the stage to the other. (2) If there is no permanent passage, a space reserved for crossing between the backcloth and the back wall.

Cruciform stage A sophisticated mechanised stage system very common in Germany. Full sized wagon stages carrying

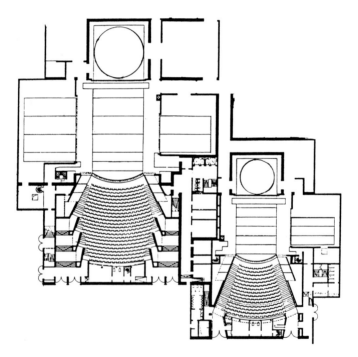

The main house (950 seats) of Darmstadt Staatstheater has a CRUCIFORM STAGE layout enabling complete settings on motorised wagons to be driven from either side, or from the rear, on to an acting area which comprises elevators framed by an adjustable proscenium. The smaller house (450 seats) is similar but has only one side stage. In both houses, the rear stage incorporates a revolve.

complete stage settings can be rolled on to the main stage area from left, right and rear.

Cue The signal that initiates a change of any kind during a performance.

Cue light Light used to signal a change, normally red for stand by and green for go.

Temporary CUE LIGHT hanging on the back of a wing flat.

Cue sheet A numbered list of actions to be initiated on cue. See also PLOT.

Curtain A large expanse of hanging fabric used to conceal and reveal action taking place behind. Often used as a con-traction when referring to HOUSE CURTAIN. (Small curtains as used on windows, etc. are usually referred to as DRAPES.)

Curtain call Acknowledgement of applause, traditionally taken by raising and lowering the house curtain or coming through its central overlapping gap. In the absence of a curtain, the lighting is blacked out and restored several times. Known as **bows** in US.

Curtain line (1) The position where the house curtain, if used, crosses the stage. With the acting area increasingly thrusting through on to the apron, this line has to be taken into account when positioning actors immediately prior to the end of an act. (2) The last line of dialogue which is the cue for the curtain to descend at the end of the play.

Curtain track See TAB TRACK.

Curtain up The beginning of the performance. Originally the raising of the curtain to reveal the stage, but often still used even when there is no curtain.

Cut (1) Contraction of CUT CLOTH. (2) To delete dialogue, action, cues, etc.

Cut border A border with an edge which is profiled rather than straight. Some of the canvas within the border may also be cut away, particularly in the case of a foliage border. Where necessary, cut portions are supported by net or gauze.

Cut cloth (Cut drop) A hanging cloth with part of the canvas cut away to show further scenery hanging behind. A series of cut cloths leading to the backcloth may be used to provide a painted perspective scene with an illusion of great depth.

Cut out Two-dimensional scenery with a shaped edge so that its silhouette is appropriate to the three-dimensional object which it represents.

Cut to cue A technical rehearsal where lengthy sections of dialogue between cues are cut to save time.

Cyclorama (Cyc) Plain cloth extending around and above the stage to give a feeling of infinite space. Term is often used for a skycloth, either straight or with limited curve at the ends. See also PLASTER CYC.

Cyclorama track A track for surrounding the stage with a cyclorama. The most sophisticated forms enable the cyclo-rama cloth, when not required, to be rolled around a cone in a downstage corner of the stage.

Dark A theatre which is temporarily or permanently closed and without performances.

Dayman Permanent full time 'rank and file' member of technical staff. Term becoming obsolete and replaced by TECHNICIAN.

Dead (1) The plotted height of a piece of suspended scenery or masking (**trim** in US). (2) Discarded items of scenery.

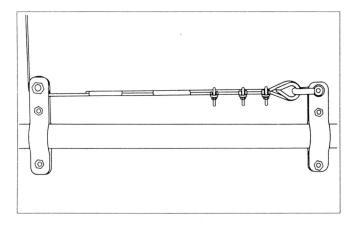

In some installations, this DEADING arrangement is used to allow small adjustments to be made to the lengths of the suspension wires so that the bars are maintained on a level dead.

Dead haul Stage or flying machinery moved by hauling a line directly by hand or motor without balance from counterweights.

Dead hung Scenery or lights on fixed suspensions which cannot be raised or lowered.

Deading cleats The lower row of cleats to which the lines of a flown piece are kept tied off so that they are on their bottom dead when lowered.

Dead line Suspension line which is fixed and not capable of being raised or lowered by the flying system.

Dead pack A pack of flats used in scenes which have already appeared and will not be repeated during the current performance.

Deck Sometimes used as jargon for the stage floor, but more correctly a false stage, probably tracked, which has been laid on top of the stage floor for a specific production.

Decor This older word for scenery has been falling into disuse with the development of the idea that the scenic environment should be an integral constituent of the production rather than merely a decorative background. See also SCENOGRAPHY.

Deep A measurement of depth, i.e. the depth of a stage or scene is described as being x feet or y metres deep.

Departments Organisational divisions of staging personnel based on specialist functions – e.g. stage, electrics, props, sound, wardrobe, etc.

Depth The dimension of a stage or scene from front (i.e. nearest the audience) to back.

Designer The person responsible for conceiving the visual environment of a production and supervising the execution of this concept. Separate designers may be employed for scenery, costume and lighting. See also SOUND DESIGNER.

Deus ex machina The introduction of a god to resolve a dramatic plot. The arrival of such a god usually involved the use of complex stage machinery.

Die Failure by an actor or production to be appreciated by the audience.

Diorama A pictorial backcloth which unrolls from one side of the stage to the other, producing an illusion that it is the action on stage that is moving rather than the backcloth. The technique was very popular in the early nineteenth century when real depth was added to painted depth by placing independent scenic pieces in front of and behind the main cloth.

This DIORAMA of Venice was painted by the great scenic artist Clarkson Stanfield for the Drury Lane, London, Christmas 1831 pantomime *Harlequin and Little Thumb*. Reviewing the first night, *The Times* commented '. . . it does not sound well to hear an invisible scene shifter call out to a pasteboard gondolier, who seemed to be rowing as well as he could, 'D-n ye, keep close to the lights'.

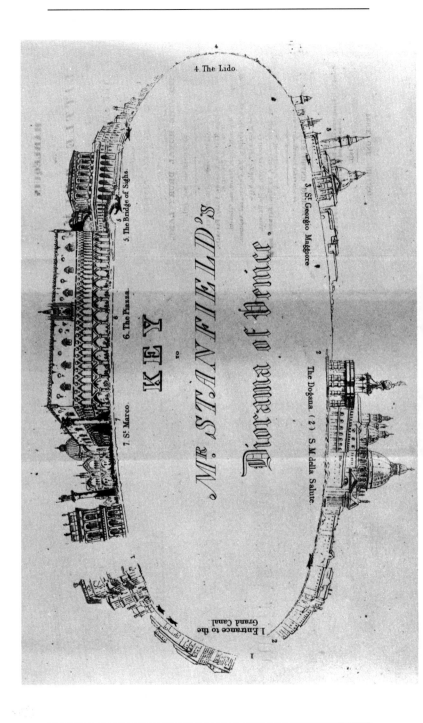

KEY
or
Mr STANFIELD's
Diorama of Venice

1. Entrance to the Grand Canal
2. The Dogana. (2) S. M. della Salute.
3. St Georgio Maggiore.
4. The Lido.
5. The Bridge of Sighs.
6. The Piazza.
7. St Marco.

Some sections were opaque and others transparent so that creative use might be made of the possibilities of gas lighting. See also PANORAMA.

Dips Small traps in the stage floor giving access to electrical sockets. (**Floor pockets** in US)

Director The person with the ultimate responsibility for the interpretation of the script through artistic leadership of the actors and the supporting production team.

Discovered Scenery or actors positioned on stage so that their presence will be revealed when the curtain rises or the lights are faded up from blackout.

Divertor A pulley block used to change the direction of a rope or wire line.

Dock See SCENE DOCK.

Dolly Small castor-wheeled base used to move heavy items of scenery during a fit-up or scene change.

DOLLY.

Dome See PLASTER CYC.

Door flat A flat with an opening into which a door frame may be inserted.

Door slam Device to provide the noise of a door being slammed. Can vary in sophistication from a complete framed door, full-size or miniaturised, to a board held against the pressure of the operator's foot by a screw-eye and rope until released to hit the stage floor.

Double (1) A piece of scenery which is used more than once, i.e. doubles between two scenes. (2) One actor substituted for another, without the audience being aware, in order to make a trick or stunt possible.

Double handling Moving scenery or equipment more than necessary because it was not properly positioned in the first instance.

Double purchase Counterweight flying system where the cradle (arbor) travels half the distance of the fly bar's travel and therefore leaves the side wall of the stage below the fly galleries clear of flying equipment. See also SINGLE PURCHASE.

Down centre (left/right) The area of the stage nearest the audience at centre (or left or right).

Downstage The area of the stage nearest to the audience.

Drapes Curtains, particularly decorative curtains rather than the flown or travelling curtains used to reveal or end a scene.

Drencher Pipe which applies water to the safety curtain in the event of fire. See also SPRINKLERS.

Dressers Wardrobe personnel who help actors with costume care and costume changing during dress rehearsals and performances.

Dressings Decorative (i.e. non-functional) items added to a stage setting.

Dress parade Prior to the first stage dress rehearsals, the actors wear each of their costumes in sequence so that director and designer can check the state of preparedness of the wardrobe, under light and preferably against a background of appropriate scenery.

Drift (1) The length of suspension wire between a counterweight bar and the top of a piece to be flown. This has to be calculated so that the bar will not show when the flown piece is in, yet mask when it is out. (2) TO DRIFT is to use drift lines to enable a flown piece to be lowered into a confined space where the ends of the flying bar would foul side scenery.

Drops Cloths lowered (or 'dropped') from the flys. (Particularly US)

Drottningholm Swedish theatre on the outskirts of Stockholm, built in 1766. Closed and undisturbed throughout the nineteenth century until rediscovered in 1921, with its original machinery and scenery preserved in a cocoon of dust. Annual summer opera seasons use this machinery for productions which enable us to experience eighteenth-century theatre technology in the performance context of operas for which it was intended.

Drum and shaft A historic method of handling flying scenery and occasionally floor traps. Lines from flown pieces wind around a shaft which is rotated by operating lines winding around a large drum mounted on the shaft. The circumference ratio of drum to shaft provides mechanical advantage and, by utilising various drum sizes, several scenic pieces can travel at different rates while operated by one person.

DRUM AND SHAFT on the grid in Drottningholm Court Theatre, Sweden.

Dry An actor forgetting the words of the script.

Dry brush Technique of brushing out wet paint with a dryish brush to give a textured finish.

Dry ice Frozen carbon dioxide added to boiling water produces a vapour which, being heavier than air, forms a mist on the stage floor. Dry ice machines incorporate water heaters and baskets to lower the dry ice pellets into the water on cue. See also FOG MACHINE.

Dry tech A rehearsal of technical cues without actors present.

DSM In the UK, the DSM (Deputy Stage Manager) is the stage management team member responsible for running the show by calling the cues which integrate all stage operations with the actors during the course of a performance.

Dutch Although Holland uses the very highest sophistication in staging technology, there is a long history of applying the adjective 'dutch' to non-orthodox and improvised equipment.

Dutchman Strip of fabric covering the join in a pair of flats which butt together (US).

Ease To lower a very little. Used particularly in the context of deading a flying piece on manual lines – i.e. 'ease your long'.

Effects Often, but decreasingly, called special effects. Essentially a simulation, usually with an attempt at realism, of an audio, visual or magical phenomenon. Effects should always be used as an integral part of the production, never just grafted on 'for effect'.

Electrics (1) All the lighting and other electrical equipment. (2) The technicians responsible for handling the lighting and electrical equipment.

Elevation A scale drawing of the front, side or rear of an object. Elevations are used to show dimensioned detail of the vertical aspects of stages and scenery.

Elevator Stage floor section which can be raised or lowered.

Entrance Any part of the stage where the actor gains access to the acting area and appears to the audience. This may be through an opening in the set or a gap in the masking. The tendency, particularly in older style theatre, for actors to appear in such a way as to draw attention to themselves is referred to as 'making an entrance'.

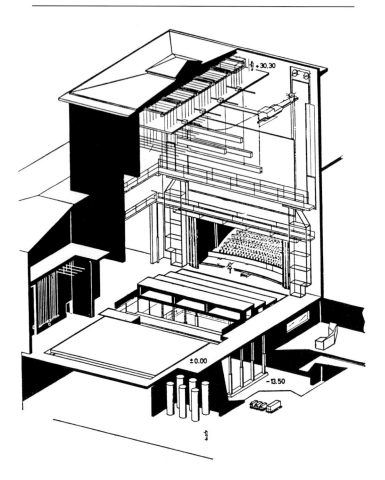

(1) (Above) Stage floor with a modular system of ELEVATORS for moving scenery and providing levels.

(2) (Above right) Section through the Paris Bastille Opera where wagon stages (B) carrying full scenery settings can be wheeled from the sides and rear or ELEVATED from below to the acting area (A).

Exteriors Scenery representing outdoor environments rather than indoor ones (interiors).

Extras Non-speaking actors, particularly those who swell a crowd scene. See also SUPER.

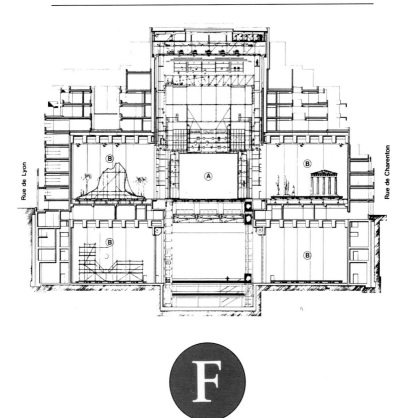

Rue de Lyon

Rue de Charenton

F

Faking Using various techniques or disguising objects to give an impression of authenticity, particularly by imitating realism.

False proscenium A portal used in the downstage area to form a specially designed frame for the action.

False stage A special stage floor laid as part of a production design to allow trucks, guided by tracks cut into this false floor, to be moved by steel wires running in the shallow void between the false and original stage floors.

Feel To pull at a tied-off line to test its tautness. Sometimes the act of pulling and letting go will release the necessary fraction of length to level a flying piece – i.e. 'feel your long'.

Felt A fabric which is pressed rather than woven. This gives it a dense texture which is particularly suitable for cushioning the sound of feet on rostrum tops where it is placed between the timber and the canvas covering.

Festoon A curtain hung in folds. See also CONTOUR CURTAIN.

Fibreglass General name for GRP (Glass Reinforced Plastic) methods of construction involving a mat of glass fibres strengthened with two-part resins which set solid.

Fire curtain Fire resistant shutter immediately behind the proscenium arch, designed to delay a backstage fire and smoke from spreading to the auditorium for long enough to allow the audience to be evacuated. Now constructed of steel, although former use of other materials still results in references to the **asbestos** (US) and the **iron** (UK).

Fire proofing Some materials are inherently fire-retardant but the majority used on the stage require to be treated with fireproofing solutions, either by impregnation or by surface coating.

Fire/flame retardant Virtually no material is impervious to flames. Fire proofing is therefore something of a misnomer: all that can be done is to retard the spread of the flames. The delay certainly has to be sufficient for the audience to escape and long enough, it is hoped, to slow down the spread sufficiently for the fire to be brought under control. Various materials are fire retardant to a greater or lesser degree and fire resistance can be improved by treatment with chemical solutions.

Fit-up (1) The initial assembly on the stage of a production's hardware, including hanging the scenery, building the trucks, etc. (2) An older name for a touring company who could adapt to playing in halls and improvised theatres of all types.

Flamebar A range of proprietary non-toxic flame retardants specially formulated for the materials used in scenery, props and costumes.

Flats Lightweight timber frames covered with scenic canvas. Now usually covered with 4mm or 6mm plywood and consequently no longer quite so lightweight. When dropped into position from the flys, known as 'french flats'.

Flipper A narrow flat hinged to a wider flat, usually either to provide stability or to form a link by filling the gap between moving and fixed parts of the scene.

Float Letting a flat fall gently to the stage floor by utilising the cushioning effect of the air trapped under its large surface area.

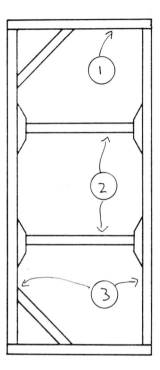

FLAT built from top and bottom rails (1), vertical stiles (3) and intermediate toggles (2).

Float trough A recessed area at the front of the stage for the accommodation of footlights.

Flog Remove dust and dirt from hanging curtains or cloths by beating them with a flogger of narrow strips of canvas attached to a wooden handle.

Floorcloth A cloth, usually painted as part of the total design, covering the acting area of the stage floor. (STAGE-CLOTH in UK)

Floor plan See GROUND PLAN.

Floor pockets Small traps in the stage floor providing access to electrical sockets for lighting (mostly US – DIPS in UK).

Flown scenery Scenery which is suspended from the flying system.

Fly bars The metal pipes to which scenery and lights are attached for hoisting (i.e. flying) above the stage.

Fly floor High working platform at the side of the stage, running from downstage to upstage, from which flying lines are handled. Sometimes called Fly Gallery.

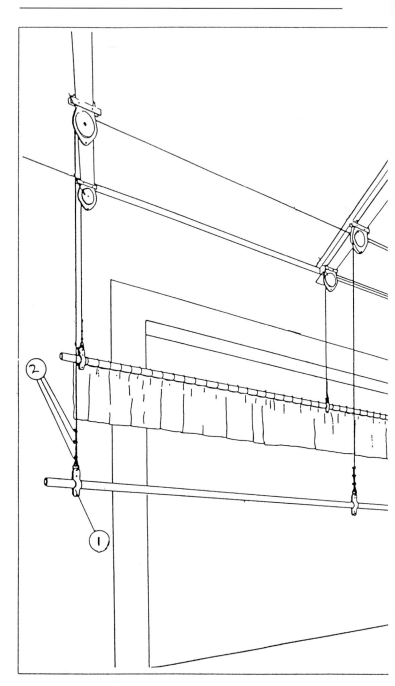

Manual FLYING SETS. Each line is attached to the bar by a hanging ring
(1) and secured with bulldog cable grips (2). These lines pass over single

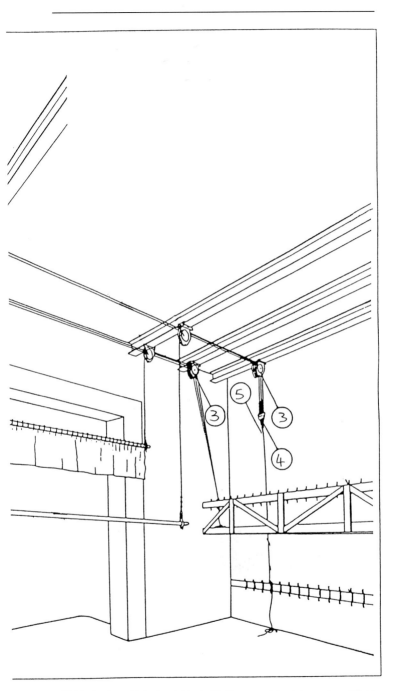

grid blocks to a triple head block (3) then are joined by a clew (4) to
provide a hauling line for each set (5).

Flying chains Short lengths of chain with a snap hook at one end used for attaching battened cloths to a fly bar.

Flying iron See HANGING IRON.

Flying set Each group of associated rope lines (short, centre and long) of a hemp flying system, or each bar of a counterweight system and its associated weight cradle (arbor) and hauling line.

Fly loft The space in the fly tower between the grid and the roof.

Flyman Technician who operates the scenery suspension system above the stage.

Fly rail Strictly speaking, the horizontal timber or steel beam carrying the cleats to which the lines for flown scenery lines are tied. But often extended to include the operational part of the counterweight frame where the lines are hauled and locked.

Flys (1) The area above the stage into which scenery can be hoisted out of sight of the audience. (2) The side galleries above the stage from which the flying lines are operated.

Fly tower High structure above the stage with machinery for hoisting scenery out of sight.

Looking up into the FLY TOWER of the National Theatre in Taipei.

Fog machine A machine which produces dense smoke by vapourising special oil or water mixtures. The vapour tends to be lighter than air and disperses upwards. See also DRY ICE.

FOH (Front of house) Everything on the audience side of the proscenium.

Fold (1) Flats which are hinged together are often described as Twofolds or Threefolds. See also BOOK FLAT. (2) Premature end of the anticipated run of a production.

Folding jack A french brace which is hinged to a flat. (US)

Folding rostrum A platform frame which is hinged to fold flat. This frame supports a separate solid top.

Foliage border A border with painted leaves. Usually cut out in an intricate pattern which is supported by net glued behind the holes in the canvas.

Foot Placing a foot against the bottom of a flat lying on the floor to stop it slipping while someone else raises it to the vertical. See also WALK IT UP.

Foot irons Right-angled strips of iron, fixed or hinged, for securing the bases of flats, ground rows, etc. to the stage floor. (US)

Found space A theatre formed within an existing building which was not originally intended for performance use.

Forestage The area in front of the house curtain on a proscenium stage. Also known as APRON.

Foul Items of scenery interfering with each other, particularly when two pieces flown close together become entangled, or a border becomes trapped on the top of a flat.

Fourth wall The invisible wall through which the audience see a play in a box set.

Four walls A theatre rental agreement providing minimum facilities and equipment. Usually involves a fixed rental payment rather than a box-office percentage.

Framed border A canvas border which is made rigid and prevented from creasing by timber framing.

Framed cloth A flown cloth which is prevented from creasing by timber framing.

French brace Non-adjustable timber brace, usually attached to a scenic flat by a pin hinge. Often swung flush to the flat on this hinge prior to packing in the wings or flying.

A flat supported by FRENCH BRACES.

French flat A scenic flat which is flown into position.

Frenchman A french flat.

Frontcloth (1) A cloth hanging at the front of the stage.

(2) A variety act which can perform in the shallow depth of stage in front of a frontcloth. See also OLIO.

Front of house (FOH) All areas of a theatre on the audience side of the proscenium. Everywhere that is not backstage or back of house.

Fullness Fabric gathered at the top of a curtain so that it hangs in folds. Masking legs and borders were formerly made in this way, although straight (no fullness) is now more common.

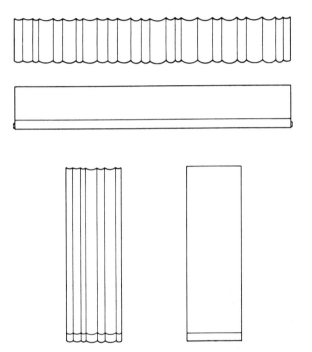

Borders and legs may be straight or the material may be gathered for FULLNESS. Pockets are usually incorporated for weighting by chain or conduit.

Full set A scene designed to utilise the full extent of the available acting area.

Full stage A scene using all the available stage depth.

Fusible link A link in a chain or wire with a low melting-point in order to release a fire curtain or open a smoke lantern (haystack) in the event of fire.

Gaffer tape Strong adhesive plastic-backed fabric tape used for a multitude of purposes – even including, in an emergency, holding the set together!

Gantry A narrow access gallery, usually at high level. See also CATWALK.

Gauze An open weave fabric which becomes transparent or solid under different lighting conditions. (**Scrim** in US)

Genie A trade name (but becoming generic) for a telescopic hoist used to raise and support rigs or technicians.

Get-in (1) Unloading a production into a theatre. (2) The door through which scenery enters and leaves the theatre.

Get-off Off-stage steps which enable actors to descend to stage level out of audience view after making an exit from a high level on the set.

Get-out (1) Dismantling a production and loading it into transport for removal from the theatre. (2) The minimum weekly box office receipts that will cover a production's expenses to the point of break even.

Ghost glide See CORSICAN TRAP.

Glass crash The sound of breaking glass, traditionally made by pouring broken glass from one bucket to another. More sophisticated glass crashes have involved sheets of glass broken on cue by weights released by an electrical solenoid.

Glaze Emulsion glaze is often used to add a lustre and form a protective coat to stage floors which have been painted as part of the production design.

Glitter Minute particles of a reflective material, such as metalised polyester film, added to scenic and costume surfaces to make them sparkle.

Glue The traditional fixative used in scenery construction is animal glue, a protein extracted from slaughterhouse remnants. In a dilute solution, known as SIZE, it is the binding agent for pigments in traditional scene painting. For most purposes, natural glue has now been overtaken by a wide range of specialist synthetic fixatives.

Glue gun A gun shaped applicator which electrically heats hot-melt glue sticks.

Go The action word for any cued change.

Grave trap A trap midstage centre, originally associated with *Hamlet*.

Green The part of the stage visible to the audience. There are many theories as to the origin of 'green', varying from green baize as a stagecloth to the rhyming cockney slang of 'stage' with 'greengage'.

Green room Room adjacent to the stage (i.e. the 'green') for the actors to meet and relax.

Grid The arrangement of wooden or metal slats above which are mounted the pulley blocks of the flying system.

Grid block A pulley block mounted on the grid to change the direction of a flying line from horizontal to vertical so that it drops between two adjacent slats.

Gridded Any flying piece which has been raised as high as possible into the flys, i.e. to the limit of travel of the set of flying lines.

Gridiron The full name for a metal grid.

Grips Stage crew members responsible for handling scenery. (US)

Grommets Protective surrounds for holes – e.g. holes cut in cloths for lacing, or holes cut in an auditorium ceiling for suspension wires.

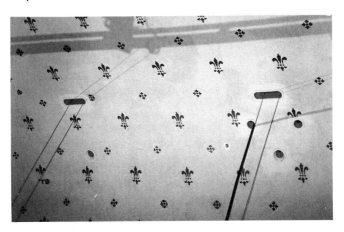

GROMMETED holes for suspending flying wires through an auditorium ceiling.

Grooves Strips of timber which guided and supported sliding wings as the scene changed in sight of the audience from the seventeenth to the nineteenth century on UK stages. The use of lower grooves fixed to the stage floor did not last as long as the upper grooves which had hinged sections enabling the flymen to drop them on to the top of large flats. Indeed the upper groove principle, reduced to a device like a garden fork, remained in some minor theatres until well into the present century. Grooves were used in early US theatres, whereas in Continental Europe the wings, guided by slots, travelled on carriages under the stage floor. See also WING CARRIAGES.

Upper GROOVES formerly used to steady wing flats. The onstage section was normally hinged, as here, to lift.

Ground cloth See STAGECLOTH.

Ground plan Scale plan showing the exact position of all items standing on the stage floor and indicating the position of items suspended above. Also known as **floor plan** (US).

Ground row A low piece of scenery standing on the stage floor, often only a couple of feet or so high.

Grummet (1) Metal guide screwed or bolted to the top of a french flat to keep in position the flying cable running from a flying iron at the bottom of the flat. (2) Also used on flats to hold the knotted end of the lash line.

GRUMMET used to guide the suspension wire on a french flat.

Guide wires Taut vertical wires threaded through rings attached to the sides of a curtain, to ensure that it does not billow up- or downstage when flying. Use normally confined to the main house curtain which is particularly susceptible to draughts caused by climatic differences between stage and auditorium.

Half A call given to the actors half an hour before they will be called to the stage for the beginning of the performance. The half is normally called 35 minutes before the advertised time of commencement. (Subsequent calls are 'the quarter', 'five minutes' and 'beginners'.)

Hallkeeper The traditional title for the person responsible for stage door security. Often called STAGE DOOR KEEPER, although the word 'security' is increasingly appearing in the job title.

Hand cue A cue signalled by dropping a raised hand sharply (raising the hand serves as the stand-by signal).

Hand line A single rope line which is pulled manually to effect an action.

Hand props Small props which are carried and handled by the actors.

Hand winch See WINCH.

Hanging (1) The theatre adjective for suspended. (2) The process of attaching each item of the flown scenery and lights to its designated set of lines for a production and balancing with counterweights where appropriate.

Hanging iron Metal strap which is screwed or bolted to the bottom of a scenic flat for attaching a hanging wire, so that the weight is taken from the bottom rather than the top where it might place undue stress on the structure of the flat.

Hanging plot List of all items suspended from the grid with the number of the counterweight or hemp set on which they are hanging, or are to be hung.

Hansen cloth/gauze A thick woven gauze used for a bleed-through where the picture in front is more important than that revealed behind. Also used as an alternative to canvas for a painted cloth when the woven texture is appropriate.

Hard Constructed from hard timber rather than soft drapes. Used mainly in relation to masking.

HANGING IRON taking the weight of a suspended french flat from the bottom. (Note the bulldog grips in this photo are the wrong way round – they should be as the drawing.)

Hauling line The operating rope of a flying system.

Haystack See SMOKE LANTERN.

Head blocks The blocks at the side of the grid, immediately above the fly floor. Their grooved pulley wheels (sheaves) change the direction of the ropes or wires from vertical to horizontal.

Header A horizontal piece of flattage which spans the verticals of flown arches, portals and similar scenery where the vertical and horizontal components are constructed and transported as separate items for bolting together on the stage prior to flying.

Heads! A warning (sometimes as HEADS UP!) to look upwards because a flown piece or empty fly bar is being lowered. When shouted anxiously (sometimes as HEADS BELOW!) it usually means that some object has been dropped – such warning inevitably being too late.

Hemp The original type of rope used for flying. The term is used generally to cover all flying systems without counterweights.

Hoisting scenery in the fly gallery of a HEMP HOUSE.

Hemp house A theatre where the flying is by heaving manually on ropes without the help of mechanical advantage from counterweights.

HOD Head of department, particularly a theatre's resident stage manager, master carpenter and chief electrician.

House The auditorium and its audience.

House border Neutral masking border immediately up-stage of the main house curtain. It may be used to mark the height of the proscenium opening for a particular show or, if a show's design includes a false proscenium, to complete the masking from the top of the header of that false proscenium.

House curtain (House tabs) The main curtain filling the proscenium opening. Usually made from a rich velour fabric and lined to improve sound and light isolation between stage and auditorium. In accordance with long standing theatre tradition, the most common colour scheme is red with gold trimming. Flying is the most common operational mode in Anglo-American theatre, although the format is usually a pair of overlapping single curtains to allow a centre entrance for acknowledging applause.

Housekeeper Supervisor of a theatre's cleaning staff.

Horse-powered pump for seventeenth-century Italian HYDRAULIC stage technology.

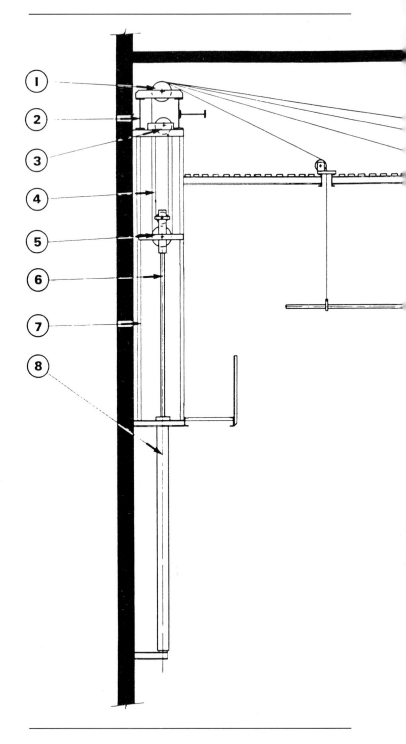

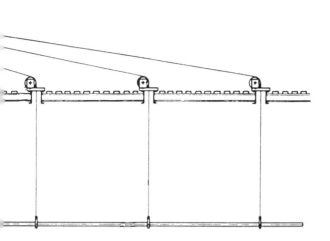

Basic structure of a HYDRAULIC flying system. Lines from the fly bar pass over a head block (1) to the top (2) of the pulley (3 and 5) and line (4) system which reduces the distance required to be travelled by the ram (6) which is supported by pulley guides (7) as it moves in and out of the hydraulic cylinder (8). The bar travel is four times that of the ram.

Hydraulics The transmission of power by fluid offers a fine degree of control that is attractive for the delicate timing of the scenic movements required on a stage. Permanent installations use hydraulics mostly for stage elevators and advanced flying systems, while individual set designs sometimes use the method to move individual items of scenery.

In Flown scenery or empty fly bars which have been lowered so that they are visible.

Industrial show A production staged to promote a manufactured product, particularly the launch of a new product to the salesmen and agents of the manufacturing company.

In one A scene played downstage in the first bay.

Inset A small scene which can be set inside a larger one without significantly dismantling the larger one.

Instrument Any stage lighting unit whether floodlight or spotlight. A US term now coming into increasing international use.

Interior A scene set indoors rather than outdoors (an exterior).

In the round Staging format where the acting area is surrounded by audience seating. Rarely round, usually rectangular or polygonal.

Iron The fire retardant safety curtain separating the stage from the auditorium. See also ASBESTOS, FIRE CURTAIN and SAFETY CURTAIN.

Island setting A self-contained scenic environment which sits in the centre of the stage, isolated from any physical connection to the wings.

Isora A plastic skycloth lit from behind.

Jack (Sometimes BRACE JACK.) A FRENCH BRACE (US).

Jackknife stage (Truck) A castored truck or full stage wagon pivoted at one corner so that it may swing on and off stage in an arc.

Jardin Stage right (actor facing the audience) in the French theatre, derived from a tradition whereby the garden was always to the right and the court to the left. Hence stage left is COUR.

Jog A narrow flat set at right angles to another flat. Helps to provide stability. Often used in interior box sets to improve the illusion of structural solidity of the corners, fireplaces, etc.

Joints The major types of timber joint used in scenery construction include:

Butt A 90° join between two timbers where the end of one rests against the side of another, held together by a triangular corner of plywood which is certainly screwed or pinned and probably glued.

Mitre A 90° join between two timbers where each end is cut at a 45° angle and butted together.

Lap A 90° join between two overlapping timbers.

Half-Lap A 90° join between two overlapping timbers where each has half its thickness cut away.

Mortice and tenon A tongue (tenon) cut in the end of one timber is gripped in a slot (mortice) cut in the side of the other timber. This is the traditional joint for constructing scenic flats to the highest professional quality but is less frequently used now that flats tend to be covered in ply rather than canvas.

Scarf Joining two timbers end-to-end by tapering the first 18 inches of each so that, when overlapped, the overall width is not increased.

Doweled A method of strengthening joints by drilling holes in the two timbers to be joined so that glued round wooden pins, known as dowels, may be inserted.

Jump in a rail To insert an extra toggle rail into a flat to provide fixing for set dressings such as pictures.

Keep alive Storing props and items of scenery in the wings or scene dock so that they are readily accessible for use on the stage.

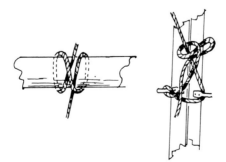

A clove hitch (left) and the lash KNOT used for tying off the lash line joining flats (right).

Kill To remove. Therefore sometimes used as an alternative to STRIKE, particularly if the piece of scenery or prop to be struck is also to be removed permanently from the production. An item which has been killed becomes DEAD.

Knots See CLOVE HITCH, TIE OFF and LASH KNOT. *See illustration on page 51.*

Knuckle The hinged joint between book flats.

Ladder Short narrow frame with several horizontal bars for hanging side lighting. Some theatres have permanent tracks bolted to the underside of the fly floors – these permit ladders to be positioned where required and moved, if desired, in scene changes.

Lantern (1) See SMOKE LANTERN. (2) Older UK term for a flood or spotlight, now overtaken by US **instrument**.

Lash knot The quick release knot used to lash flats together. (*See illustration on page 51.*)

Lash line The rope line used for tying two flats together. See CLEAT LINE and THROW LINE.

Lead Occasionally used as an alternative to iron for counterweights in order to reduce bulk.

Leading bobbin The tab track bobbin to which the onstage (i.e. 'leading') edge of a curtain is tied.

Left Actor's left, facing the audience.

Leg drop Leg (US).

Legs Vertical strips of fabric used mainly for masking, either decorative or neutral.

Let in (Bring in) To lower in scenery from the flys.

Levels Acting areas higher than the stage floor.

Lifting jacks Castors which, on operation of a lever, take the weight of scenery for movement.

Lifts Older term, falling into disuse, for ELEVATORS.

Limit switch Device which detects that a motorised unit such as an elevator or fly bar has reached its predetermined

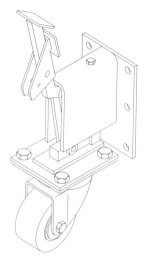

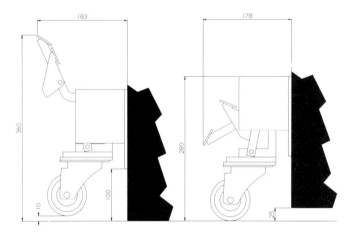

Wheeled castor (above) with LIFTING mechanism which allows a truck to sit firmly on floor (below left) until jacked up (below right) for wheeling. (Triple E Unijack™ System)

limit of travel (i.e. its DEAD or TRIM) and halts it by switching off its power.

Linear motors In this type of induction motor, the moving and stationary parts are linear and parallel so that a current causes motion along a line. This makes linear motors very suitable for moving scenery on overhead tracks. Collecting its power and control data from conductor rails mounted along the top of the track, the motor carriage runs along the track pulling curtains or flats behind it. This eliminates

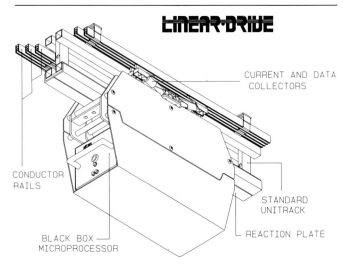

LINEAR MOTOR (Triple E Ltd).

trailing wires and enables the moving scenery to traverse complex curved paths. A wide range of speeds is possible and the motor starts, stops and reverses instantly on command.

Lines   The wires or ropes on which scenery and lights are suspended.

Live   (Sometimes ALIVE.) Any prop or item of scenery which has still to be used, or will be used again, during the current performance.

Load   (1) Placing the appropriate counterweights in the cradle (arbor) to balance the weight of the object to be flown. (2) The quantity of scenery, props or electrics is often measured in truck 'loads'.

Load in/out   US terms for getting a production into and out of a theatre. See BUMP IN/OUT, GET-IN and GET-OUT.

Loading gallery   A working platform high (near the grid) in the fly tower where counterbalancing weights are added to the cradles (arbors) of counterweight lines while their bars are at their lowest level of travel (approximately waist high above the stage floor).

Lock rail   The rail carrying the rope locks which prevent unwanted travel of correctly counterweighted fly bars.

Loft   Another name, mostly US, for the fly tower – i.e. contracted from fly loft.

Long   The line furthest from the fly floor of the three lines of a manual flying hemp set.

Make fast Tying-off a rope line but implying a rather more permanent tie than is implied by the phrase 'tying off'.

Make-off To tie lines to a cleat, particularly the ropes of a flying system, but sometimes also used for securing the lines which lace flats together.

Marie tempest Door closing device named after the famous actress.

Marking Placing small discreet marks on the stage floor (temporarily with tape, more permanently with paint) to aid the positioning of scenery and props during a change.

Mark-out Sticking coloured plastic tapes to the rehearsal room floor to indicate the ground plan of the scenery.

Maroon Electrically fired pyrotechnic which provides an explosive bang with loudness dependent upon the size of maroon selected. Normally fired in a bomb tank.

Masking Neutral material or scenery which defines the performance area and conceals the technical areas.

Master carpenter Senior member of the scenery staff in the theatre. Also senior carpenter in the workshops.

Mechanist Alternative name (particularly Australasia) for a technician responsible for handling scenery.

Mimic display A miniature pictorial indication of the position of the moving items in an equipment system. Most such displays are now presented on video screens but some earlier technology arranged its knobs and switches so that their positions not only denoted the means of operation but also provided a mimic. For example, the shape of some contour curtains was set by moving a row of individual slider controls, one for each of the operating motors, and a chain linking those controls provided a mimic of the curtain shape.

Model The designer's scale model of a stage setting. The standard scale is 1:25, a metrication of the old half inch to the foot (1:24), although 1:50 is sometimes used for particularly large stages.

T034087

Model box (1) The model stage which houses the scene design model. Often just a wooden baseboard with a black cardboard cut-out proscenium and a simple frame to support flying pieces – giving it the proportions of a box. (2) Proprietary name for a computer visualisation and drafting system based on Autocad.

A MODEL BOX in the paint room at Covent Garden, London in 1889.

Modular stage A stage floor constructed of identically sized sections which can be removed singly or in groups to allow entrances, traps or machinery to be placed in any position.

Monkey stick A length of cane taped to the lash line of a flat to enable the line to be hooked over a cleat without the need for throwing. This reduces the noise and, with inexperienced hands, increases the certainty of achieving a fast scene change.

Mouldings Three-dimensional timber pieces, such as skirting boards and architraves, added to scenic-flats as an alternative or supplement to two-dimensional painting in order to increase reality.

Mule block A pulley block used to change the direction of a rope or wire line (US). See DIVERTOR.

Multiple set A scenic environment comprising several locations. The collection of acting areas may be constant throughout the performance or altered by additions and subtractions to a basic standing set.

Net A stiff wide mesh open-weave fabric used to support elaborately cut-out canvas scenery such as foliage borders.

Noises off Sound effects relating to a happening offstage, i.e. outside the stage environment visible to the audience.

NVQ All areas of stage technology are included in the UK system of National Vocational Qualifications which is being developed for all industries. Standards are set by the theatre industry itself and skill assessment takes place in the workplace.

Off An actor who misses an entrance.

Off stage The masked areas to the sides and rear of the acting area.

OISTAT (Organisation Internationale des Scenographes, Techniciens et Architectes de Theatre). International forum for theatre architects, designers and technicians. Most national associations are affiliated and act as hosts, in rotation, for OISTAT's specialist commissions. The PQ (Prague Quadriennial) exhibitions are a major influence in stimulating developments in scenography.

Olio (Oleo) Traditional US name for a painted cloth hanging downstage, flown by rolling from the bottom. Used for playing a scene or a vaudeville act, while the next scene was being set behind. The scene in front was often known as an Olio

Act or Olio Scene. Akin to the UK use of FRONTCLOTH both for the scene and for a variety act capable of playing in the restricted space.

On stage (1) The acting area as seen by the audience. (2) A call to actors or crew to come to the stage area.

On stand by In a state of readiness to carry out an action on cue.

On the book The member of the stage management team (normally the DSM in the UK) responsible for recording actor moves in the prompt book during rehearsals then calling the cues during the performances. Also prompts if necessary.

OP Opposite Prompt side of the stage – i.e. stage right (actor's right when facing the audience). See also PS.

Open stage A stage with audience seated on more than one side and no framing by a proscenium arch.

Operating line A rope, particularly one in a flying system, which is handled to activate the required movement.

Orchestra lift An elevator to adjust the height of an orchestra pit or parts of it. Also used to convert the pit into additional seating or a forestage.

Orchestra shell Scenic surround, often including a ceiling, placed on stages to improve the acoustic for concerts which do not use microphones.

Out To raise up into the flys ('out' of sight). The opposite of IN (to lower down 'in' to sight).

Out front The auditorium.

Outrigger (1) A stabilising side support for a mobile vertical access ladder such as a tallescope. (2) A castored frame attached to the back of a scenery item to aid movement in a scene change. (US)

Overhaul Pulling against the force of the counterweights to lower a fly bar beyond the point where its load is resting on the stage floor and consequently no longer in balance with the counterweights. This has to be done, for example, if flats, flown parallel to the front of the stage, have to be set at an angle to it. It may be necessary to attach an independent line, possibly with block and tackle, to the counterweight cradle; or to deploy a CARPET HOIST.

Pack Flats stored vertically, resting against each other.

Paint Traditional scene paint is a mix of dry pigments in a bonding medium of heated glue size. This size has been largely replaced by new synthetic media, and much of today's scenery is painted with vinyl acrylic paints which are sold as a thick paste to be thinned with water to an appropriate consistency. See also ANILINE DYES.

Paint floor Large horizontal floor area on which cloths and scenery can be laid for painting. There are often galleries to allow the artists to view the progress of work from a distance. This is the standard scenic painting method in much of Central Europe.

Painting scenery on the FLOOR in the 'continental' tradition.

Paint frame Vertical frame to which cloths or flats can be nailed for painting. The traditional paint frame, often at the back of the stage, has a winch for raising or lowering the frame to allow the artists, standing on a fixed platform, to work on appropriate sections of the cloth. With some modern paint frames, the frame is static and the artists work

Painting on a movable FRAME from a fixed platform.

on small motorised platforms which move vertically and horizontally.

Panic bolt A method of locking an outwardly opening emergency exit door so that it cannot be opened from the outside but is easily opened from inside by pushing a horizontal bar at waist height.

Panorama A vast scenic painting, either stationary or moving between vertical rollers from one side to the other. Apart from use as a background in stage productions, panoramas were a popular exhibition entertainment of the late eighteenth and early nineteenth centuries. See also DIORAMA.

Painting on a fixed FRAME from a moveable platform.

Papier-mâché A mix of shredded paper and paste, flexible and easily moulded when wet but hard when dry, still used for making props although overtaken to a considerable extent by newer materials.

Parallel Platform with folding hinged base and separate top. (US) Called FOLDING ROSTRUM or just ROSTRUM in UK.

Pass door Door near the proscenium arch, leading directly from backstage to the auditorium. Usually narrow and made of steel because it is a break in the fire wall intended to retard the spread of any stage fire to the auditorium. Custom restricts the use of this door during performance to a very small number of authorised people.

Peephole stage See PICTURE FRAME STAGE.

Pelmet A semi-permanent border set in the proscenium arch, in front of the house curtain. In addition to its decorative function, it serves to complete the masking of the house curtain on both its top and bottom deads (trims). Sometimes called HOUSE BORDER, although, strictly speaking, this label should be reserved for the first masking border immediately behind the house curtain.

Perches Lighting positions immediately behind the proscenium arch on each side of the stage. In older theatres, there may be a series of platforms in these positions. Increasingly, however, such platforms are being removed to leave clear wing space for trucked scenery to be manoeuvred.

Periaktoi Triangular scenic elements which are rotated to show alternative faces for different scenes. They may consist of three flats simply lashed together or be complex built trucks.

Permanent set A scenic environment which does not change during the performance. The complete set may be permanent or the majority of the structure may remain while minor elements are added and subtracted.

Personal props Small items such as keys, letters, money, etc., carried by actors on to the stage.

Physical production The costs involved in providing all the stage environment for a new production, i.e. set building and painting, furniture and set-dressings, props, costumes, wigs.

Piano dress Rehearsal in costume and with all technical facilities but using a piano as a substitute for orchestra so that director, cast and crew can concentrate on movement and technical problems rather than musical ones.

Picture frame stage Sometimes called PEEPHOLE STAGE. Theatre form where the proscenium makes a very positive division between stage and auditorium.

Pilots Low intensity or blue lights which do not illuminate the acting area but allow actors and technicians to move about safely in the wings. See also WORKING LIGHTS.

Pin hinge Hinge with removable pin used to join two pieces of scenery together (one half of the hinge is on each piece of scenery).

Pin rail A horizontal timber or steel beam through which cleats, modelled on ship's belaying pins, are slotted for tying off manual flying lines. (Mostly US)

PROP money specially printed for a production.

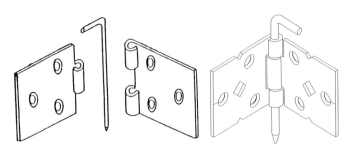

The standard PIN HINGE (left) as upgraded by Triple E (right) has lines to assist accurate location and a centre hole for an optional coach bolt for extra strength, while the bigger diameter pins are tapered for easy assembly.

Pipe (Pipe batten) The bars on which scenery or lights are flown. (Mostly US)

Pipe clamp See BARREL CLAMP.

Pit (1) Area in front of the stage for musicians. Originally at floor level but now usually sunk and often extending underneath the stage. (2) In the Georgian theatre, the pit was an audience seating area at ground floor level. In the Victorian theatre, the front rows became the orchestra stalls and only the rear area was designated pit.

Pit lift see ORCHESTRA LIFT.

Pivot point Hole drilled in the stage floor to receive a pin which provides an axis about which a truck may be rotated.

Places please Warning given by stage managers in US that the actors should take their opening positions on stage as the curtain is about to rise.

Plaster cyc A permanent cyclorama, plaster surfaced, built as the rear limit to the stage's acting area. Sometimes called DOME. Such permanent cycloramas were a feature of serious theatres in the earlier part of the century, particularly in Central Europe where they were curved to wrap around at least the rear sides of the acting area, and frequently also domed over the top. Many had holes, accessed from the rear, for tiny lamps to simulate stars. See also CYCLORAMA.

Platform A unit for providing an acting surface above stage level. (US) Called ROSTRUM in UK.

Plot A listing of preparations and actions required during a performance. Each staging department prepares such plots as are required by that department's individual members.

Point hoist A single flying line positioned exactly where

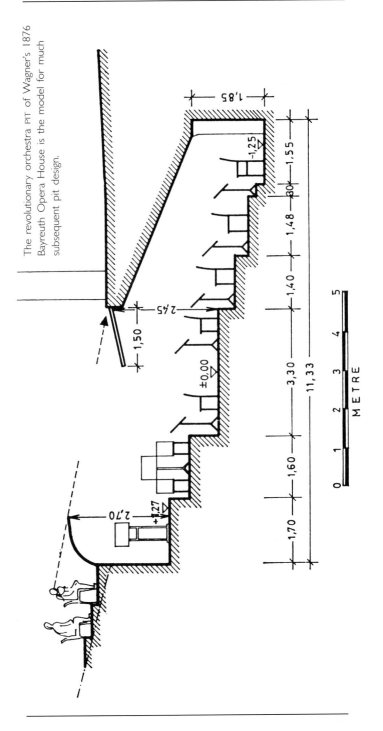

The revolutionary orchestra PIT of Wagner's 1876 Bayreuth Opera House is the model for much subsequent pit design.

1,85

-1,25

1,55

30

1,48

1,40

2,45

1,50

±0,00

3,30

11,33

1,60

2,70

+1,27

1,70

0 1 2 3 4 5

METRE

65

required in the grid by the use of diverter blocks and driven by an electric motor.

Polyester Synthetic resin which becomes solid on interaction with a hardener chemical. Very strong construction material when used in conjunction with glass fibre matting. See FIBREGLASS.

Polyethylene See POLYTHENE.

Polypropylene A synthetic, with ropes as its main stage application.

Polystyrene A synthetic which can be used in a hard moulded form, but on stage is normally used as a lightweight expanded foam which can be relatively easily carved.

Polythene The normal name for polyethylene products. Possibly the most common of the synthetic polymer 'plastic' materials, whether as solid moulded objects or flexible textiles.

Polyurethane Available in most formats including sheet, both flexible and rigid, as a resin for moulding and as a foam for texturing.

Polyvinyl acetate (PVA) A resin used in paints and adhesives.

Polyvinyl chloride (PVC) Flexible thin sheet plastic which can be transparent, translucent or opaque, either clear or coloured.

Portal Framed masking border bolted to framed masking legs. Portals may be neutral but are usually decorated.

Masking PORTALS in use for a Christmas pantomime.

Powered flying (1) Electric or hydraulically powered winches may be used for flying. In their more sophisticated form, these are single point hoists which can be grouped in any desired combination for synchronised control through a computer. (2) Motors may be added to a counterweight flying system: the counterweights still balance the load but the pulling is by motor rather than by hand.

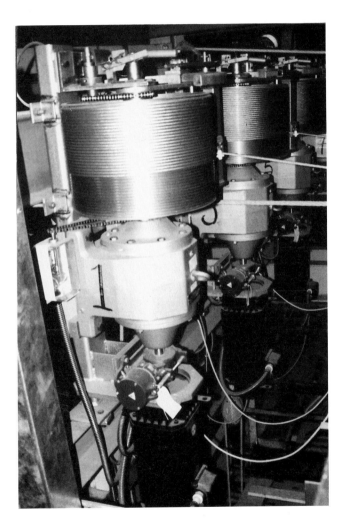

For POWERED FLYING, motor driven hoists are mounted on each side of the grid of the Royal Opera House, Covent Garden, London. Vertical winding drums enable the wires to be run directly without diversion to the point hoist pulleys on the grid. (ASA Brown Boveri System)

Control desk for the ASA Brown Boveri System of POWERED FLYING.

Practical Anything (particularly props and electrics) which has to work realistically rather than merely look realistic.

Preset Anything which is positioned in advance of its being required – such as props placed on the set before the performance; or a scene set behind a frontcloth, to be revealed when the cloth is flown.

Preview A performance given prior to the formal first night when the critics are invited. The audience understand and accept that the production is still being polished and are normally compensated for this by reduced seat prices.

Priming Treating newly covered canvas flats with a thin coat of size or paint to make the canvas taut and fill its pores.

Producer Formerly (and sometimes still in opera) the person who directs the actors. Now the packager who brings together script, theatre, production team, possibly the star(s) and certainly the money.

Production desk Temporary rehearsal table with communications equipment for the use of director, lighting designer and other members of the production team in the auditorium. Today's theatre, with its teams of production specialists, has a marked tendency to proliferate such desks which have a habit of sprouting computer screens.

Production manager Responsible for the technical preparation, including budgeting and scheduling, of new productions.

Profile Shaped piece, usually of plywood, added to a scenery flat as an alternative to a straight edge.

Progress shots Sequence of photographs of stage settings and actors used to assist accurate revival of productions.

Prompt book Master copy of the script or music score, containing all actor moves and technical cues, used by the stage management to control the performance.

Prompt box Masked opening in the centre of the downstage edge of the stage to allow a prompter's head to be

PROMPT BOX.

A performer's view of the PROMPTER. (Toulouse-Lautrec, reproduced with permission of Museu de Arte de São Paulo)

visible and audible to the performers. Until fairly recently, prompt boxes were regularly used in opera houses where the prompter was a member of the music staff hissing the words just before they were sung. With increasing rehearsal time, the need for prompting has declined and permanent prompt boxes have disappeared with the footlights where they were once a central feature. However, in most opera houses, there is still a trap which can be opened to form an instant prompt box.

Prompt copy See PROMPT BOOK.

Prompt corner The position immediately behind the proscenium, traditionally on the actor's left side of the stage, from where the stage manager runs (i.e. controls) the performance by calling the cues. See also BASTARD PROMPT.

PROMPT DESK. (Northern Light)

Prompt desk The desk, equipped with communication facilities, from where the stage manager runs the performances. Traditionally fixed to the wall, but increasingly mobile and capable of being plugged-in at either side of the stage.

Prompter In a play, the stage manager who runs the show is also responsible for prompting any actors who 'dry' (i.e. forget their words). But an opera is driven by the orchestra so, if a singer forgets a line, prompting after the dry is too late. Consequently, every line has to be hissed out in advance by a member of the music staff from a little box in the centre of the footlights. But prompting is now only used in opera productions when there has been few rehearsals or an emergency cast change.

Property master Traditional title for the head of the props department, although the title Property Manager is increasingly used.

Props (Properties) Furnishings, set dressings, and all items large and small which cannot be classified as scenery, wardrobe or electrics.

Prop table Table at the side of the stage where props are laid ready for use. Often marked off into labelled sections for each prop.

PROP TABLE.

Proscenium (Pros., Pros. arch) The division between audience and stage in the traditional form of theatre where the audience sits in a single block facing the stage. The proscenium takes many forms from a definite arch, not unlike a picture frame, to an unstressed termination of auditorium walls and ceiling.

Proscenium doors Doors at the side of the stage, built into the proscenium arch of eighteenth-century theatres. The actors normally made their entrances through these doors rather than through the scenery.

PS Prompt side of the stage – stage left (actor's left when facing the audience). See also OP.

Pull rod A timber or metal rod attached to a truck so that

Picture frame PROSCENIUM arch with house tabs at Newcastle Theatre Royal.

it may be positioned by an unseen technician pulling or pushing from the wings.

Pusher Jargon for a scene shifter, particularly the second of a two person team where one walks in front with the

PROSCENIUM DOOR at the Theatre Royal in Bury St Edmunds. (Architect: William Wilkins, 1819)

leading edge of the flat while the other lifts (and 'pushes') the rear edge.

Pyrotechnics Bombs, bangs, flashes, etc., usually fired electrically.

Q The normal way of writing CUE.

Quarter The call ('Quarter of an hour, please') given to warn actors that beginners will be called to the stage in fifteen minutes. Normally given twenty minutes before the advertised time of the start of the performance.

Quick change An actor's fast change of costume.

Quick change room A permanent small dressing room adjacent to the stage kept available for quick costume changes. Or a temporary changing 'room', built from scenery flats on the side of the stage.

Rag Jargon for house curtain.

Rail (1) The FLY RAIL. (2) Horizontal cross timbers at the top and bottom of the frame of a scenery flat. (*See illustration of flat on page 33.*) (3) Lighting position on the front of an auditorium balcony. (US)

Rake Inclined stage floor. Older stages had, and many still have, a permanent rake, rising at half an inch in every foot (i.e. 1 in 24). Today's scene designs often include a temporary raked floor over part or all of the stage.

Rearfold A track which pulls a curtain from its off stage rear edge rather than, as standard, from its on stage leading edge.

Register Something which the audience notice is said to 'register' with them. There are times when some particular aspect of the design and technology of a production has to be slightly emphasised or highlighted to ensure that it will register.

Repertoire A form of organisation where two or more

productions alternate in the course of a week's performances. See also STAGIONE.

Repertory A form of organisation, usually with a permanent company of actors, where each production has a run of limited length. At any time there is normally one production in performance, another in rehearsal, and several in varying degrees of planning.

Repetiteur Pianist and vocal coach in an opera house.

Resident stage manager Title given, mainly in touring theatres, to the master carpenter. Responsible to the theatre manager for the technical staff and the building, and to the touring manager for providing performance facilities.

Returns (1) Subsidiary flats set at an angle to the main scenic flats, usually to complete the masking. These may be, for example, flats running offstage, parallel to the front edge of the stage, to terminate upstage to downstage walls; or masking flats angled downstage from the offstage ends of portals. (2) A statement of ticket sales produced by the box office manager nightly, and summarised weekly.

Reveal (1) Timbers, often built as a separate frame, fastened to the back of an opening, such as a door or window, to give an illusion of thickness in scenery constructed from flats. (2) To expose to audience view by such means as raising a curtain, moving scenery in sight, fading up lights from blackout or bleeding through a gauze, etc.

Revolve A turntable stage. Larger revolves (diameter wider than proscenium opening) allow complete scene changes, while smaller ones (diameter less than proscenium opening) allow partial scene changes and choreographed movement with actors dancing against the movement, or even bicycling against it.

Rigging Hanging and assembling the stage hardware (scenery, lights, etc.) for a production.

Right Actor's right, facing the audience.

Ring up/down Cueing the curtain up and down, particularly at the start and end of the performance. In the eighteenth century, the prompter gave the cue by a bell.

Rise and sink A Victorian method of revealing a new scene by raising the top half of the scene in front into the flys and lowering the bottom half into the cellar. Used in pantomime for transformations.

Riser (1) The vertical of a step (the horizontal is a TREAD). (2) A microphone on a stand which can be winched to any

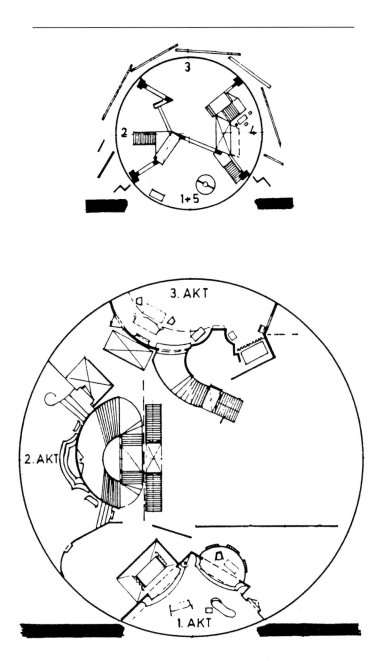

(Above) Most REVOLVES have a diameter approximately the same as the width of the proscenium opening and are particularly suitable for movement in view of the audience. (Below) A few opera houses have revolves so large that only a small segment is viewed through the proscenium: such revolves can handle changes of complete sets.

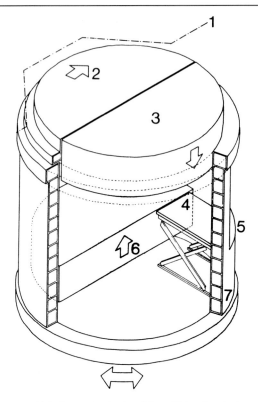

The REVOLVE which forms the basis of the Olivier thrust stage of the Royal National Theatre in London. The broken line (1) indicates the position of the front edge of the stage. Either of the twin elevators (3 or 6) can be at stage level while the other is dropped to the basement for scene changing through the door (5) to the scissors lift loading platform (4). The space vacated by either lowered elevator is filled by a disc (2) which can revolve independently or lock to the stage while the entire drum frame (7) revolves below on wheels at basement level.

required height by hand or motor through a small trap at the front of the stage. (Now mostly superseded by radio microphones.)

Road manager (Roadie) A touring technician with one-night stands, particularly pop groups.

Roll ceiling The canvas is attached to front and back timber battens on which it can be rolled for storage and transportation. See also CEILING and BOOK CEILING.

Roller Wide round timber used with rope lines to roll a cloth from the bottom when there is insufficient height for conventional flying. See also TUMBLER.

Rope lock A handbrake which clamps on the hauling line of a counterweight set and prevents a balanced load from moving in either direction.

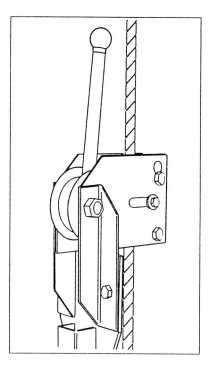

ROPE LOCK.

Rosin (Resin) box A shallow box, positioned by the door from the dressing rooms to the stage, containing resin for dancers to dip the soles of their shoes as a precaution against slipping. A traditional practice not normally required, and better avoided, with modern vinyl dance floors.

Rostrum A portable platform usually in the form of a collapsible hinged framework with separate top.

RSJ (rolled steel joist) Key load bearing members of the stage and fly tower structure.

Rumble truck Not the cause of a noisy scene change but a device used in the days when sound effects were produced physically rather than reproduced electronically. A weighted truck with irregular wheels was a constituent (along with cannon ball runs, drums and iron sheets) of rumbling thunder. (**Rumble cart** in US)

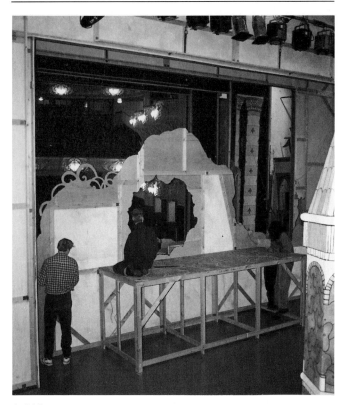

A folding ROSTRUM.

Run (1) A sequence of performances of the same production. (2) Moving a vertical scenery flat by grasping it (one hand low, the other high) by the stile of the leading edge and, facing the direction of travel, raising it only just clear of the stage floor. The rear bottom corner (often called the Heel as opposed to the leading Toe) is allowed to slide along the stage floor. For wider and heavier flats an additional person, known as a pusher, balances and pushes the rear stile.

Runners A pair of curtains parting at the centre and moving horizontally, particularly those used in a downstage position in variety and revue productions.

Running order The sequence of events in a production – a summary of the play without dialogue.

Running plots These list actions of setting and striking scenery and props to be carried out during each scene change or on cue within scenes. See also CHECK PLOTS.

Run out Platform over the orchestra pit with steps down to the auditorium. Sometimes used to allow actors to enter from the auditorium in performance, but more frequently for the production team to have access to the stage from the auditorium during rehearsals.

Safeties US term for the various safety restraints (chains, cables, ropes, etc.) used to reduce possible accidental damage from falling loose items, including tools.

Safety curtain Fire resistant curtain running in vertical tracks fixed to the proscenium arch, designed to contain any stage fire within the stage area in order to gain time for the audience to escape. See also ASBESTOS, FIRE CURTAIN and IRON.

Safety factor Margin allowed for occasional excess stress in calculating the rated maximum load of ropes, wires, etc.

Sandbag (1) Canvas bag filled with sand and fitted with a tie-ring for weighting unused sets of hemp lines so that they can be lowered easily to the stage. (2) A large sandbag may be used as a temporary counterweight to balance the load in hemp flying.

Sandwich batten Two lengths of timber screwed together with the top or bottom of a cloth sandwiched between.

Sash cord Slender, but strong, rope line as used in sash windows. Useful for joining cleated flats together and similar situations which involve strain rather than supporting a load.

Scene change Complete or partial alteration of the physical environment on the stage to indicate a different location or a passage of time.

Scene dock High-ceilinged storage area adjacent to the stage.

Scene paint See PAINT.

Scene shifters Technicians responsible for moving scenery.

Scene shifting The changing of scenery, particularly when carried out manually with the curtain down.

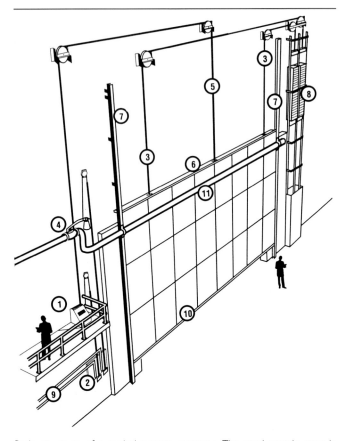

Basic structure of a typical SAFETY CURTAIN. The steel curtain runs in smoke-lock guides (7), has smoke plates at the top (6) and a smoke pad (10) at the bottom. It is suspended on lines (3) from a balancing counter-weight cradle (8) and raised by another line (5) from a motorised hoist (1). Descent is controlled by a hydraulic arrester. Primary control is from the prompt corner (2) with secondary control lines (9) to the stage door. The drencher pipe (11) is fed with water through a valve (4).

Scene shop A workshop area for making and painting scenery.

Scenographer The international term for the designers who provide the visual environment for the actor. Implies a theatre where the environment is an integral constituent of the production rather than a decorative addition.

Scenography The international term for stage design, particularly when the stage environment, costumes, light and sound play a major part in a production concept and are totally integrated with it. See also DECOR.

SANDBAG used to weight an unused hemp line.

Schedules Very few possibilities of technology can be explored or demonstrated in a rehearsal room. Since technical stage time is always short, even shorter than money, careful scheduling of the available time is essential. The schedules which work tend to be those that are agreed rather than imposed – even if that agreement is reached with the inevitable reluctance.

Scrim Gauze. (US)

Section A cross-sectional drawing of stage and scenery in the vertical plane along the centre line. Normally shows all suspended scenery on its top and bottom deads (trims).

Segue Musical term for an immediate follow on. Often used for any kind of immediate follow on.

Seizing Binding the end of a wire rope to prevent the strands unlaying.

Self-sustaining winch A winch with a device to prevent the cable from running if the winding force on the handle is removed. For small winches this is often a pawl which drops by gravity into the teeth of a ratchet on the drum.

A SELF-SUSTAINING WINCH which maintains its position through friction. For added safety under load, a line would normally be tied from the handle to the adjacent cleat.

Sensation A spectacular scene in the Victorian theatre, usually including particularly impressive effects and transformations.

Serge A wool material with a dead light-absorbing surface which makes it very suitable for neutral masking.

Set back Reverse a scene change to the previous scene during rehearsal, often because the change did not go according to plan.

Set (Setting) (1) The scenery. (2) To place scenery or props in position. (3) Several flying lines used as a group.

Set piece A unit of free-standing scenery, normally three-dimensional.

Setting line A line, usually just upstage of the house curtain and parallel to the front of the stage, from which all positions for the scenery are measured.

Sharkstooth A thick woven gauze where the thread is more prominent than the holes.

Sheave The pulley wheel, grooved to take a line, in a block.

Short The line nearest to the fly floor of the three lines in a normal hemp flying set.

Shot bag A bag filled with lead shot for weighting curtains. See also SANDBAG.

Show curtain (tabs/cloth/gauze) A painted front curtain which is part of the production design and replaces the theatre's house tabs except, perhaps, when the audience is arriving and departing.

A SHOW CURTAIN painted on gauze so that the opening scene can be revealed by a bleed.

Show deck See FALSE STAGE.

Showman Part-time member of staff engaged for performances only.

Side arm Horizontal timber hinged to the top of the off-stage edge of a wing. A curtain leg hanging from this side arm completes the masking but can be swung briefly aside to allow scenery to be moved on and off the stage.

Side tails Masking legs in the wings to complete the

masking from seats with extreme sightlines. May be hung from side arms, from the fly gallery or from a bar running up and downstage in the wings.

Sightlines Lines drawn on plan and section to indicate limits of audience vision from extreme seats, including the front and back rows, side seats and seats in galleries.

Sill iron A narrow metal strap across the bottom of a gap (e.g. a door arch) in a flat to complete the structure where the flat sits on the stage floor.

Single purchase Counterweight flying system where the

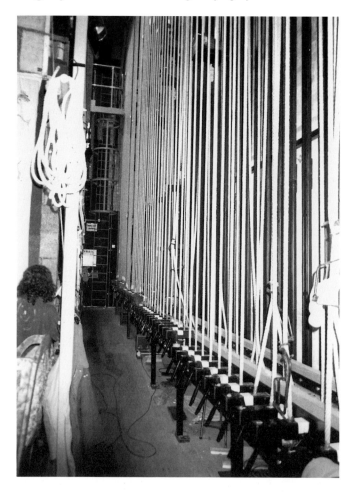

The fly rail of a SINGLE PURCHASE counterweight system. Control in this particular theatre is at stage level, although it is more usually from a fly gallery.

cradle travels the same distance as the fly bar. The counter-weight frame therefore occupies the full height of the side wall of the stage. See also DOUBLE PURCHASE.

Sitzprobe Opera house term for a rehearsal where the cast sing but do not act.

Size Animal glue used as the bonding medium for pigment mixtures in traditional scene painting.

Sizing Priming newly canvassed flats, prior to painting, by treating them with a thin solution of size.

Skin ply Very thin (2mm) plywood used as cladding in the construction of curved scenic elements such as pillars. A thicker ply (4mm to 6mm) is used to clad flats as an alternative to the traditional canvas.

Skip Heavy duty wheeled basket, with hinged lid, used for storage and transportation of props and costumes.

Skycloth A cloth painted pale blue to represent the sky.

Slapstick Pair of thin timber laths, separated at the handle by a spacer, traditionally used by clowns as a weapon which makes a noise without hurting. Still used in schoolroom scenes of Christmas pantomimes. Origin of the type of humour bearing the name.

Slash Shiny foil strips hanging from a bar and giving the appearance of a metallic cloth slashed into a series of vertical strips about 2 inches or 5mm wide.

Slider The section of stage floor which is slid under the adjacent timbers to provide an opening in the stage for a trap to be used.

Slip stage A large truck capable of carrying a complete scene and filling all or most of the full proscenium width. Guided on tracks in a false stage floor on its movement from parking in the wings. See also CRUCIFORM STAGE, WAGON STAGE.

Sloats Narrow slots which could be opened across the width of a Victorian timber stage to allow narrow scenery, mostly two-dimensional ground rows, to ascend from the basement below.

Slots Slots in the stages of eighteenth- and nineteenth-century Central European stages through which flats were inserted into the basement carriages by which wing changes were effected during the scene changes in sight of the audience. For the UK and US system, see GROOVES.

Smoke lantern (Slots, Vents) A structure above the grid which is designed to open in the event of fire and create a draught to suck the flames upwards. Louvres, slots or windows are designed to open by gravity when a lever is operated, rope cut manually or a fusible link melts. The glass of black painted windows will also break under heat.

Smoke lobby Space between two sets of doors, forming a barrier to the passage of smoke from one area to another.

Snap hook Forged metal loop, completed by a spring 'gate'.

Snap line Chalk covered cord pulled tight and sprung against the stage floor to mark a temporary line, particularly the setting line.

Snatch lines (Chains) Short lengths of rope or chain used to fix scenery to the bars (pipes) of the flying system. (US)

Snow bag Length of multi-slit canvas suspended between two sets of lines which, on agitation, release paper or polystyrene 'snow' which flutters to the stage.

Softs Masking which is curtains rather than flats.

Song sheet A flown rectangle of cloth painted with the words of a song which the audience are invited to join in singing. Still traditionally used by the star in virtually every Christmas pantomime production as part of a frontcloth scene to cover the change into spectacular scenery and costumes for the finale.

Sound designer The person responsible for planning and supervising the executing of all electronically originated or processed sounds in a production.

Sparge pipe The pipe (also known as DRENCHER) which applies water to the safety curtain in the event of fire.

Spattering Flicking paint from a brush so that it lands on the surface as a series of small splashes.

Spike (1) To mark, with paint or tape on the stage floor, the agreed positions of scenery and props. (2) To fix with nails.

Spot block A pulley block, additional to those for the normal sets of lines, placed on the grid for a special purpose.

Spot line A temporary line dropped from the grid to suspend something in an exact special position.

Sprinklers Fire fighting system with devices which automatically release water under conditions of excessive temperature rise. See also DRENCHER.

A pantomime SONG SHEET from front and back.

Staff director Member of the production department in a repertoire theatre responsible for maintaining the standard of a production, including revivals and cast changes. Usually was the director's assistant during the original rehearsals for the production.

Stage The floor of the acting area.

Stage brace Angled support for scenery. The standard adjustable-length brace hooks into a screw-eye on the flat and is either weighted to the floor or attached to it by a special large stage screw. See also FRENCH BRACE.

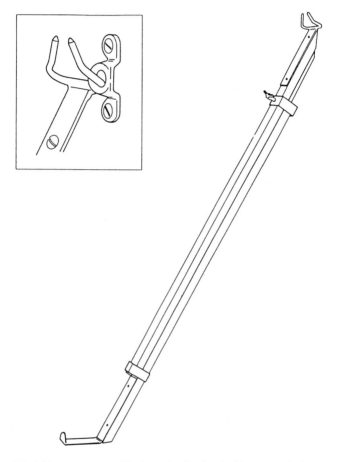

Adjustable STAGE BRACE. The brace is often hooked into a standard screw eye rather than the brace eye shown here.

Stagecloth Canvas cloth, neutral or painted as part of the production design, covering the stage floor. Also called FLOORCLOTH.

Stage crew Technicians responsible for scenery handling.

Stage directions Instructions which supplement the dialogue in a script.

Stage director Formerly the senior member of the stage management team but a title now rarely used in order to avoid confusion with the director.

Stage door Backstage entrance used by actors, crew and production staff.

Stage door keeper See HALLKEEPER.

Stagehand Member of the stage crew responsible for moving scenery at stage level.

Stage house The stage floor and all the space above and below it from basement to grid.

Stage left Left-hand side of the stage when facing the audience. See also PS and COUR.

Stage manager The person in overall control of the performance with responsibility for signalling the cues that co-ordinate the work of the actors and technicians. Some of this responsibility is delegated to the deputy stage manager (DSM) and assistant stage manager (ASM). See also ASM, DSM, RESIDENT STAGE MANAGER.

Stage right Right-hand side of the stage when facing the audience. See also OP and JARDIN.

Stage screw A large screw with a handle for fixing braces to the stage floor as a firmer alternative to weights.

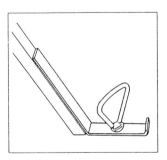

STAGE SCREW.

Stage wait An interruption to the flow of the performance caused by an actor drying or being off, or by a problem with a scene change.

Stage weight A cast iron weight used to keep the bottom of a brace in position on the stage floor.

Stage whisper An actor speaking as if whispering but in a way that can still be heard by the audience.

Stagione A form of repertoire based on a very small number of productions in performance at any given time. Each production is given intensive rehearsal followed by a few performances close together before being placed in storage for a similarly rehearsed revival at a later date. See also REPERTOIRE and REPERTORY.

Stand by (1) The warning that a cue is imminent. (2) In a state of readiness to carry out an action on cue.

Standing Scenery ('standing set') or lights ('standing lights') which do not change during the performance.

Standing by (1) Ready to respond to a cue. (2) Reply by a crew member to the stage manager's verbal warning to stand by for a cue.

Staple gun Tool for driving the wire staples which now tend to be used for many fixings, including floorcloths and as an alternative to tacks for attaching canvas or ply to flats.

Star cloth A black cloth with tiny points of light, formerly produced by strings of lamps of Christmas tree decoration size but now mostly by fibre optic threads.

Star trap A small square trap, just large enough to allow an actor to be speedily projected on a counterweighted platform through the stage floor from below. The surface is cut into small hinged triangular sections in the shape of a star which open as the actor passes through, then immediately fall back into place. See also BRISTLE TRAP.

Stile The vertical timbers of the frame of a scenic flat. (*See illustration of a flat on page 33.*)

Stock scenery Flats, rostra and steps constructed in standard sizes so that they are suitable for re-painting for re-use.

Stop blocks Small blocks of wood screwed to the stile of a flat to help make a positive join with an adjacent flat when there is 270° between faces.

Stop cleats Small flat metal cleats screwed to the stile of a flat to help make a positive join with an adjacent flat when there is 90° between faces.

STAR TRAP.

Strike To dismantle a scene and remove it, or props, from the acting area.

Strip When a standing set is erected for a long run, any noticeable joints may be covered (stripped) by pasting a narrow bandage of thin material over the join and painting to match.

Sugar glass A substitute for real glass in situations where it is required to break without inflicting injury. See also BREAK-AWAY.

Super Contraction of supernumerary. An extra actor with no dialogue who fills up the stage, particularly in crowd scenes.

Surround Curtains used to mask the back and sides of the stage (i.e. to 'surround' the acting area).

Swag To drape curtains or borders in looped formations.

Swatch (1) Small book of samples of materials, particularly fabrics or filters. (2) Costume drawing with fabric samples pinned to the paper.

Swimming For light entertainment productions, practical swimming pools have been built on stages, often with mirrors to enable the ground floor audience to see. But swimming, whether by Wagner's Rhinemaidens or by the shipwrecked Dick Whittington, is more usually simulated with the aid of flying wires.

SWL (Safe working load) The maximum safe operational load that can be applied to equipment. This should be specified by a qualified engineer and is usually subject to regulations and limited by insurance cover.

(Above) SWIMMING Rhinemaidens at the Bayreuth premiere of *Das Rheingold*.

(Right) SWIMMING Rhinemaidens at Covent Garden, London in 1936 were flown from above and steered from below. [*Tatler* drawing in the Theatre Museum.]

Tabs Originally 'tableaux curtains' which drew outwards and upwards, but now generally applied to any curtain including vertically flying front curtains (e.g. house tabs) and, especially, a pair of horizontally moving curtains which overlap at centre and move outwards from centre.

Tab track Track with centre overlap for suspending and operating horizontally moving curtains.

Tag A line of dialogue or an action which marks the climax of a scene or a sequence within that scene, particularly a joke. Tags are often the trigger for light or fly cues.

Take out Instruction to the fly crew to hoist a flown piece out of sight, as in 'Take out the backcloth' or 'Take out 37'.

Tallescope Alloy vertical ladder on an adjustable wheeled base.

Teaser Masking border, usually black or matching the house curtain, hanging immediately upstage of the house curtain. With the tormentors, forms an adjustable masking inner proscenium frame. Mainly a US term – HOUSE BORDER in UK.

Technical director (administrator) Co-ordinates and budgets the work of all the technical departments.

Technical rehearsal Known as the 'Tech', the stopping rehearsal when actors and stage technology are integrated for the first time.

Technician Member of the stage operational staff.

Theatre-in-the-round A form of staging where the audience totally encircle the acting area.

Thickness piece A piece of timber or canvas intended to give an illusion of depth to an item of otherwise two-dimensional scenery.

Threefold See BOOKFLAT.

Throw line Rope line (sash cord thickness) permanently attached to one flat and thrown over a cleat on an adjacent flat to lash them together by lacing across between screws

TALLESCOPE.

set into the stiles of both flats. (In what is surely one of the earliest examples of technical theatre education, stage carpenters replaced the locks on the doors of their domestic outside toilets with lines and cleats to ensure that their sons would acquire an essential skill to enable them to follow in father's footsteps.)

Thrust Form of stage which projects into the auditorium so that audience are seated on at least two sides.

Thunder sheet Suspended sheet of flexible metal with handles at the bottom by which it can be shaken to simulate the sound of thunder.

'With the greatest respect, Mr Van Dyke Brown, the THUNDER SHEET in your great classic book on scene painting and effects would produce a better sound if it had two handles.'

Tie off To make fast flying lines or cleat- lines. See also KNOTS.

Toggle Horizontal timber providing cross-bracing to a flat between the top and bottom horizontal rails. (*See illustration of flat on page 33.*)

Topping and tailing Cutting out the dialogue and action between cues in a technical rehearsal.

Tormentors Narrow masking flats adjacent to the proscenium and at right angles to it.

Transformation An instant scene change. Often effected by exploiting the varying transparency of gauze under different lighting conditions, or by instant swivelling of scenery.

Trap Section of the stage floor which can be opened for access to and from the understage area. See also BRISTLE TRAP, CORNER TRAP, GRAVE TRAP, STAR TRAP.

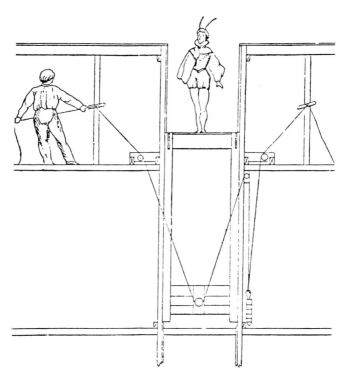

Counterweighted TRAP.

Trap room Area under the stage providing access to traps. Also called CELLAR.

Travellers Curtains which move on or off stage by means of a track ('tab track' in UK, 'traveller' in US) operated by pulling on offstage lines.

Traverse (1) A form of staging where the audience sit on

Acrobatic artistes were able to use TRAPS to project themselves on to the stage with great velocity. (George Conquest as the Ogre with his son as Puss in *Puss in Boots* at the Crystal Palace, London in 1873.)

two sides of a stage – so that the stage runs through the audience. (2) A curtain that runs across the stage.

Tread The horizontal of a step (the vertical is the RISER).

Treadmill A moving band of stage floor by which scenery or actors can be positioned. Actors can walk against it, moving but remaining in the same position.

Trick line A line, invisible to the audience, used to operate an illusion. Nylon fishing line is often used.

Trim The height above stage level of a hanging piece of

Horse running on a Drury Lane, London TREADMILL.

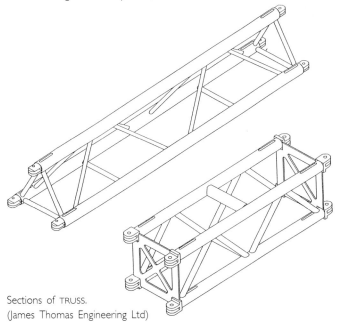

Sections of TRUSS.
(James Thomas Engineering Ltd)

scenery or masking. Mainly US (the equivalent in Britain is one of the meanings of DEAD).

Trim chains Short lengths of chain with snap hooks used to suspend scenery from flying pipes. Varying the link into which the snap hook is inserted permits some adjustment to the trim (dead).

Trip (1) TUMBLE. (US) (2) Using a second set of lines to pull hanging scenery away from vertical. (US)

Truck Castored platform on which a scene or part of a scene is built to facilitate scene changing.

Truss A framework of alloy bars and cross-bracing (usually of scaffolding diameter) providing a rigid structure.

Tumble (1) Flying a cloth from the bottom as well as from the top when there is insufficient height to fly in the normal way. (2) Alternatively, the second set of lines may be attached to a timber batten halfway up the cloth.

Tumbler The timber roller on which a cloth is tumbled.

TUMBLE flying of a cloth with a mid-cloth batten at the Tivoli Pantomime theatre in Copenhagen.

Turnbuckle A device for increasing a wire's tension by turning a sleeve which draws together a pair of eye bolts with opposing left-handed and right-handed threads.

Turn over Restoring packs after a performance so that the flats are in the correct order for the next performance.

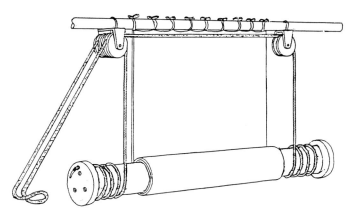

TUMBLING a cloth by rolling it from below (viewed from behind)

Turntable Revolving stage or, perhaps more strictly, the floor of that revolving stage.

Twin revolves A pair of turntables with their perimeters meeting on the centre line. Each revolve changes the scenery on its own half of the stage.

Twofold See BOOK FLAT.

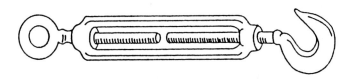

A TURNBUCKLE as used for straining the wire to trim the dead of a fly bar.

Up centre (left/right) The areas of stage furthest from the audience at centre (or left or right).

Upstage The part of the stage furthest from the audience.

USITT (United States Institute for Theatre Techno-logy) The American forum for theatre architects, designers, technicians and educators to exchange information and opinions. There are commissions for every specialist area of technology and a major conference is held each year in a different theatrical city across the nation. USITT is the American Centre for OISTAT.

U.V. Ultraviolet light from which harmful radiations have been filtered out. An invisible light under which specially treated materials fluoresce on an otherwise blacked-out stage. Can be used for scenery marks which need to be located during a scene change in a blackout.

Vacuum forming Texturing thermoplastic sheet for scenic surfaces by softening under heat and drawing over a mould by creating a vacuum.

Valance (1) Drape hung above a window to conceal the curtain rail. (2) Drape hung above, and in front of, the house curtain to mask its top when lowered in and bottom when flown out. (Mainly US)

Vamp Spring loaded flap in scenery which closes immediately an actor has made an entrance or exit through it.

Variety A traditional variety performance, known as a variety bill, comprises a sequence of acts which follow each other without any linking material between them. There may be one or several performers in each act which is a self-contained mini-production with its own script, music, costumes and props. Scenery is cloths and drapes from the venue theatre's stock.

Vaudeville The US equivalent of VARIETY.

Velcro Material used as a temporary fastener. Two surfaces of minute nylon hooks and loops cling together until tugged apart.

Velour Fabric with a surface pile of fibres raised from the underlying material. It has something of the rich plushy quality associated with velvet.

Vignette Older term for a stage setting which selects a few representative realistic details to indicate a more complete environment.

Virtual reality A computer-aided design system where, by wearing highly sophisticated goggles, it is possible to experience the illusion of entering into the designed environment.

Vision gauze A fine gauze (scrim) where the holes are more prominent than the thread.

Vomitory An entrance through the seating tier in an auditorium with a steep rake. May be used for actors to appear suddenly within the audience before making their way to the stage.

Wagon Castored platform on which scenery is built to facilitate changing. (US term – TRUCK in UK)

Wagon stage Mechanised stage where the scenery is moved into position on large sliding platforms as wide as the proscenium opening. The platforms have dedicated parking areas to the sides and rear of the main stage. These areas can be isolated by shutters which are fire retardant and provide acoustic isolation.

Walk it up Raising a flat from lying horizontal on the floor to standing vertical. One person places their foot to stop the bottom of the flat sliding while another lifts the top from the floor then walks towards the first person, using their hands to raise the top increasingly to vertical.

Wardrobe General name for the costume department, its staff, and the accommodation that they occupy.

Wardrobe maintenance The division of the wardrobe department responsible for day-to-day cleaning, pressing and running repairs.

Wardrobe plot Actor-by-actor, scene-by-scene inventory of all the costumes in a production, with a detailed breakdown into every separate item of each costume.

Warning Instruction to stand by for a cue which is imminent.

Waves Heaving seas are now usually a matter for optical projection or, if something more symbolic is stylistically appropriate, undulating fabric. However eighteenth-century

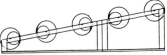

(Above) Ships on the stage of Drottningholm Theatre sail through an eighteenth century sea of five rotating rollers with moulded WAVES. Long section (above) Cross section (below).

ships sailed through realistic seas of rollers spiralling in eccentric orbits.

Weights See COUNTERWEIGHTS and STAGE WEIGHT.

Whipping Binding the ends of a fibre rope to prevent the strands from untwisting.

Wiffenpoof A piece of fur which is pulled by an invisible fishing line through a series of hooks attached to the scenery. By timing a sequence of short runs operated consecutively, the wiffenpoof can make quite complex runs. The trick is still frequently used in Christmas pantomime where the wiffenpoof makes a habit of leaping out of pies and being chased along the front of the stage before runnning around a portal and disappearing down an actor's trousers. Such a sequence would normally require at least four separately operated runs.

Winch Device for gaining mechanical advantage by winding lines around a drum turned, usually through gears, by hand or motor. See also CAPSTAN WINCH.

Wing carriages During the eighteenth and nineteenth centuries, scene changes in Continental Europe were effected in sight of the audience by substituting sets of wings

Rats running down a flat using the WIFFENPOOF - principle.

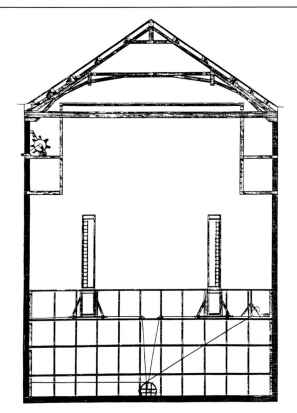

Classic French WING CARRIAGES.

mounted, through stage floor slots, in basement carriages moved simultaneously by a shaft and drum system. For the UK and US system see GROOVES.

Wing men An older term, still occasionally heard, for the two halves of the stage crew, one on each side of the stage, handling scene changes.

Wings (1) The technical areas to the sides of the acting area. (2) Scenery standing where the acting area joins these technical areas.

Wipe A single curtain moving across the stage from one side rather than a curtain from each side overlapping at the centre.

Wipe track A track on which a single curtain (known as a WIPE) can be drawn across the stage.

Working drawings Dimensioned scale drawings showing sufficient detail for workshop construction.

Working lights Stage lights independent of the main dimming system, switched from the prompt corner but sometimes with an overriding switch in the control room in case the prompt corner forgets to switch off after a scene change.

Working side The side of the stage (right or left) from where the fly lines are operated.

Zarges An A-frame ladder where the rungs are extended beyond the apex.

Using a ZARGES ladder.